GED® Test Prep HERO

Quick, Time-Saving Study Guide, Full Length Practice Tests, and 7 Proven Strategies for your GED Exam

Taylor J. Collins

Welcome to Your GED Exam Success Journey!

Congratulations on taking the first step towards achieving your educational goals! You've chosen the right book to guide you through your GED exam preparation, and we're excited to support you every step of the way.

Exclusive Online Exam Simulator Access

As an added bonus, gain exclusive access to our online exam simulator. This powerful tool offers additional full-length practice exams with real-time feedback and explanations, providing you with an authentic exam experience. **Go to page 144 to access our exclusive online exam simulator.**

Thank you for choosing "GED Test Prep Hero"

Let's get started on the path to your future success!

Disclaimer:

GED® is a registered trademark of the American Council on Education (ACE) and administered exclusively by GED Testing Service LLC under license. This material is not endorsed or approved by ACE or GED Testing Service.

Trademark Acknowledgments:

All trademarks, service marks, product names, and logos appearing in this book are the property of their respective owners. Use of these marks does not imply any affiliation with or endorsement by them.

Table of Content

INTRODUCTION

Welcome to Your GED Success Journey

Welcome to GED Test Prep Hero! We're thrilled that you've chosen this guide as your companion on the journey to obtaining your GED diploma. Preparing for the GED can be a daunting task, but with the right strategies, resources, and mindset, you can conquer the exam and open new doors to your future.

This book is designed with you in mind—whether you're balancing a job, family commitments, or other responsibilities, we understand that your time is valuable. That's why we've created a quick, time-saving study guide that focuses on delivering the most essential information and effective study techniques. Our goal is to help you maximize your study time and pass the GED exam, without unnecessary stress.

Throughout this guide, you'll find comprehensive explanations of each subject area, practical tips, and proven strategies to tackle the exam confidently. We'll walk you through full-length practice tests, providing detailed answer explanations to ensure you understand every concept. Additionally, we've included a dedicated section on overcoming test anxiety, helping you maintain a calm and focused mindset during your preparation and on test day.

At GED Test Prep Hero, we believe in your potential to succeed. This book isn't just about passing an exam; it's about empowering you to achieve your educational and career goals. With determination and the right tools, you can transform this challenge into an opportunity for growth and success.

Let's embark on this journey together. Open the pages with confidence, embrace the learning process, and take the first step towards becoming a GED Test Prep Hero. Your future is waiting, and it starts right here, right now. Welcome to your path to success!

How to Use This Book

This book is structured to provide you with a clear, efficient, and stress-free path to GED success. Here's how you can make the most of it:

Comprehensive Coverage

Each chapter is dedicated to one of the four main sections of the GED test: Reasoning Through Language Arts (RLA), Mathematical Reasoning, Science, and Social Studies. Within each chapter, you'll find detailed explanations of the key concepts, practical tips, and example questions with thorough answer explanations. This ensures that you gain a deep understanding of the material and are well-prepared for any type of question you might encounter on the exam.

Flexible Study Plans

Recognizing that your schedule might be tight, we've included flexible study plans to help you organize your preparation time effectively. These plans are designed to fit into your busy life, allowing you to study in short, focused sessions that maximize retention without overwhelming you. Tailor the study plans to match your personal pace and availability, ensuring that every minute you spend studying is productive and efficient.

Proven Strategies

In the "7 Proven Strategies" chapter, you'll discover effective techniques for mastering the GED test. These strategies are based on real-world experience and data, helping you approach each section of the test with confidence and competence. Whether it's time management tips, critical reading techniques, or methods for solving math problems, these strategies are your toolkit for success.

Practice Tests

Full-length practice tests are a crucial part of your preparation. This book includes two comprehensive practice tests that mirror the format and difficulty of the actual GED exam. After completing each test, review the detailed answer explanations to understand any mistakes and reinforce your knowledge. These practice tests will help you build stamina, improve your timing, and reduce test-day anxiety by familiarizing you with the exam's structure.

Overcoming Test Anxiety

One of the biggest challenges in taking the GED is managing test anxiety. We've dedicated a chapter to techniques for overcoming this hurdle, providing practical advice on relaxation methods, breathing exercises, and long-term anxiety management strategies. By addressing this crucial aspect of test-taking, we aim to help you maintain a calm and focused mindset, both during your preparation and on the exam day.

Additional Resources

At the end of the book, you'll find an appendix with a glossary of key terms and study plan templates. The glossary will help you understand important concepts quickly, while the study plan templates offer a structured approach to your study sessions. Use these resources to enhance your learning experience and stay organized throughout your preparation.

To get the best results, we recommend following these steps:

1. **Start with the Introduction**: Familiarize yourself with the GED test structure and the content of each section.

2. **Develop Your Study Plan**: Use the flexible study plans to organize your study schedule.

3. **Dive into Each Section**: Work through the chapters dedicated to each test section, using the example questions and explanations to reinforce your understanding.

4. **Implement the Strategies**: Apply the proven strategies to your study routine to improve efficiency and effectiveness.

5. **Take the Practice Tests**: Complete the full-length practice tests to simulate the exam experience and identify areas for improvement.

6. **Manage Test Anxiety**: Practice the techniques for overcoming test anxiety to ensure you remain calm and focused.

By following this structured approach, you can confidently prepare for the GED exam, knowing you have the tools and strategies needed to succeed. This book is your guide to achieving your goals—use it wisely, stay committed, and watch your hard work pay off.

Overview of the GED Test

The GED (General Educational Development) test is designed to measure the skills and knowledge equivalent to a high school diploma. It consists of four subject areas: Reasoning Through Language Arts (RLA), Mathematical Reasoning, Science, and Social Studies. Each section tests a specific set of skills and knowledge, ensuring that you have a comprehensive understanding of fundamental academic concepts.

Reasoning Through Language Arts (RLA)

The RLA section is divided into three parts: reading comprehension, writing, and grammar. You will be required to read and understand both literary and informational texts, analyze the arguments and evidence presented, and demonstrate your ability to write clearly and effectively. The writing portion includes an extended response, where you must write an essay based on a given prompt. This section also tests your grammar and punctuation skills, ensuring you can communicate effectively in written English.

Mathematical Reasoning

The Mathematical Reasoning section assesses your ability to solve problems using algebraic and quantitative skills. This section is split into two parts: the first allows the use of a calculator, while the second does not. You'll encounter questions on topics such as equations, expressions, geometry, and basic arithmetic. Your ability to interpret and analyze data presented in graphs and tables is also tested. This section emphasizes real-world problem-solving skills, ensuring you can apply mathematical concepts to everyday situations.

Science

The Science section evaluates your understanding of life science, physical science, and earth and space science. This section includes questions that test your ability to read and interpret scientific information, conduct scientific investigations, and understand scientific principles and concepts. You'll encounter questions that require you to analyze experiments, understand data presented in charts and graphs, and apply scientific reasoning to solve problems. The Science section is designed to test your ability to think critically and understand the natural world.

Social Studies

The Social Studies section covers history, geography, civics and government, and economics. You'll be tested on your ability to read and understand historical texts, interpret maps and graphs, and analyze political and economic information. This section includes questions on significant events in U.S. history, basic principles of government and civics, fundamental economic concepts, and geographical literacy. Like the other sections, Social Studies emphasizes the ability to think critically and apply knowledge to real-world scenarios.

Test Format and Timing

Each section of the GED test is timed, and you'll need to manage your time effectively to complete all the questions. Here's a breakdown of the time limits for each section:

- **Reasoning Through Language Arts (RLA)**: 150 minutes (2 hours and 30 minutes), including a 10-minute break.

- **Mathematical Reasoning**: 115 minutes (1 hour and 55 minutes).

- **Science**: 90 minutes (1 hour and 30 minutes).

- **Social Studies**: 70 minutes (1 hour and 10 minutes).

The test is primarily computer-based, but in some locations, a paper-based option may be available. The questions include multiple-choice, drag-and-drop, hot spot (select an area), fill-in-the-blank, and extended response formats. Each section is scored on a scale of 100 to 200, with a passing score of 145 for each section.

Scoring and Results

To pass the GED test, you must achieve a minimum score of 145 on each of the four subject tests. Scores range from 100 to 200, and the test is designed to measure your proficiency in each subject area. A score of 145-164 indicates high school equivalency, while a score of 165-174 suggests college readiness, and a score of 175-200 may qualify you for college credits.

Importance of the GED

Earning your GED is an important milestone that opens doors to further education and better job opportunities. It is recognized as an equivalent to a high school diploma by colleges, universities, and employers across the United States. Successfully passing the GED demonstrates your commitment to your education and your ability to meet rigorous academic standards.

By understanding the structure and expectations of the GED test, you can better prepare yourself for success. This book will guide you through each section, providing the knowledge, strategies, and practice you need to achieve your goals. Let's dive in and start preparing for your GED journey with confidence and determination.

Your Path to Success

Embarking on the journey to earn your GED is a significant step toward a brighter future, and we're here to guide you every step of the way. Your path to success involves a combination of strategic planning, effective study techniques, and a positive mindset. This book is designed to provide you with all the tools you need to navigate this journey with confidence and achieve your goals.

The first step on your path to success is setting clear, achievable goals. Understand why earning your GED is important to you—whether it's for career advancement, higher education, or personal fulfillment. Defining your motivation will help you stay focused and committed throughout your preparation. Write down your goals and refer to them whenever you need a reminder of why you're on this journey.

A well-structured study plan is essential for effective preparation. Begin by assessing your current knowledge and identifying areas where you need improvement. Use the flexible study plans provided in this book to organize your study time efficiently, allocating specific times for each subject and sticking to your schedule as closely as possible. Remember, consistency is key, and even short, focused study sessions can be incredibly effective when done regularly.

In this book, you'll find seven proven strategies designed to help you tackle each section of the GED with confidence. These strategies are tailored to maximize your efficiency and effectiveness, ensuring that you make the most of your study time. From mastering time management during the test to developing critical reading skills and overcoming test anxiety, these strategies will equip you with the techniques needed to succeed.

Practice is a crucial component of your preparation. The full-length practice tests included in this book are designed to simulate the actual GED exam, providing you with a realistic testing experience. Take these practice tests under timed conditions to build your stamina and improve your time management skills. After completing each test, review the detailed answer explanations to understand your mistakes and learn from them. This practice will help you become familiar with the test format and boost your confidence.

Maintaining a positive mindset is vital for your success. It's natural to feel overwhelmed at times, but remember that every step you take brings you closer to your goal. Celebrate your progress, no matter how small, and use setbacks as opportunities to learn and grow. Surround yourself with supportive people who encourage you and believe in your potential. Keep your end goal in sight and remind yourself of the benefits that come with earning your GED.

Test anxiety is a common challenge, but with the right techniques, you can manage it effectively. This book includes a dedicated section on overcoming test anxiety, offering practical advice on relaxation methods, breathing exercises, and long-term strategies to stay calm and focused. Implement these techniques during your study sessions and practice tests to build your confidence and reduce anxiety on the actual test day.

Take advantage of the additional resources provided in the appendix, such as the glossary of terms and study plan templates. These tools will enhance your learning experience and keep your study sessions organized and productive. Be prepared to adapt your study plan as needed. If you find that certain techniques or schedules aren't working for you, don't hesitate to make adjustments. The goal is to find a study routine that fits your lifestyle and maximizes your learning.

By following the guidance and strategies outlined in this book, you are setting yourself up for success. Trust in your ability to learn and grow, and remain dedicated to your goal. The journey to earning your GED is a significant milestone, and with determination, preparation, and the right resources, you can achieve it. Your path to success starts here, and we're excited to be a part of it. Let's get started and make your GED dreams a reality!

CHAPTER 1
QUICK AND EFFECTIVE PREPARATION

Preparing for the GED test doesn't have to be overwhelming or time-consuming. By adopting a strategic and flexible approach, you can maximize your study time and ensure that you're fully prepared for each section of the exam. In this chapter, we will guide you through creating a study plan that fits your schedule, optimizing your study time, and utilizing quick and focused study techniques that will help you absorb and retain information efficiently.

Creating Your Flexible Study Plan

The foundation of effective GED preparation is a well-structured study plan tailored to your individual needs and schedule. A flexible study plan allows you to integrate study sessions into your daily routine without feeling overwhelmed. Here's how you can create a personalized study plan that maximizes your efficiency and sets you up for success.

Step 1: Assess Your Starting Point

Before you can create a study plan, it's important to understand where you currently stand. Take a diagnostic pre-test to identify your strengths and weaknesses across the four GED subjects: Reasoning Through Language Arts (RLA), Mathematical Reasoning, Science, and Social Studies. This will help you allocate more time to areas where you need the most improvement.

Step 2: Set Clear and Achievable Goals

Establish specific, measurable goals for each week of your study plan. For example, you might aim to complete a certain number of practice questions, master specific concepts, or finish a full-length practice test. Setting clear goals will keep you motivated and on track.

Step 3: Design a 4-Week Study Plan

Here's a detailed 4-week study plan that covers all four subject areas, ensuring you're thoroughly prepared for each section of the GED exam. Adjust the plan as needed to fit your schedule and learning pace.

Week 1: Reasoning Through Language Arts (RLA)

- **Day 1-2**: Reading Comprehension – Focus on understanding literary texts and informational texts. Practice identifying main ideas, themes, and details.

- **Day 3-4**: Writing and Text Structure – Study different types of essays and their structures. Practice writing short essays.

- **Day 5-6**: Grammar and Punctuation – Review basic grammar rules and punctuation. Complete practice exercises.

- **Day 7**: Practice Test – Take a practice RLA test to assess your understanding and progress.

Week 2: Mathematical Reasoning

- **Day 1-2**: Algebra – Focus on equations, expressions, and solving for variables. Practice with sample problems.

- **Day 3-4**: Geometry – Study properties of shapes, measurements, and theorems. Work through practice questions.

- **Day 5-6**: Arithmetic – Review percentages, proportions, and basic arithmetic operations. Complete practice exercises.

- **Day 7**: Practice Test – Take a practice math test to evaluate your skills and identify areas for improvement.

Week 3: Science

- **Day 1-2**: Physical Science – Study basic concepts in physics and chemistry. Focus on understanding key principles and terminology.

- **Day 3-4**: Life Science – Review fundamental concepts in biology, including cellular biology, genetics, and ecosystems. Practice interpreting scientific data.

- **Day 5-6**: Earth and Space Science – Learn about the Earth's structure, weather patterns, and the solar system. Complete related practice questions.

- **Day 7**: Practice Test – Take a practice science test to gauge your comprehension and progress.

Week 4: Social Studies

- **Day 1-2**: U.S. History – Study significant events and figures in U.S. history. Focus on understanding timelines and cause-and-effect relationships.

- **Day 3-4**: World History – Review major events and movements in world history. Practice analyzing historical texts and documents.

- **Day 5-6**: Geography and Civics – Study geographical concepts and the basics of U.S. government and civics. Complete practice exercises.

- **Day 7**: Practice Test – Take a practice social studies test to assess your knowledge and readiness.

Step 4: Incorporate Regular Review Sessions

Regular review is essential for retaining information. Set aside time each week to review previously studied material. This helps reinforce your learning and ensures that you don't forget important concepts.

Step 5: Stay Flexible and Adjust as Needed

Life can be unpredictable, and your study plan should be flexible enough to accommodate changes. If you miss a study session, don't stress—simply adjust your plan and make up for it when you can. The key is to remain consistent and committed to your study goals.

Step 6: Utilize Study Tools and Resources

Make use of the various study tools and resources available in this book, such as practice questions, full-length tests, and detailed answer explanations. These resources are designed to help you deepen your understanding and improve your test-taking skills.

By following this structured yet flexible study plan, you can efficiently cover all the necessary material and approach the GED exam with confidence. Remember, consistency and dedication are your greatest allies on this journey. Let's dive into the specifics of optimizing your study time and employing quick, focused study techniques in the next sections.

Optimizing Study Time

Maximizing the effectiveness of your study sessions is crucial when preparing for the GED, especially if you have limited time. By implementing smart strategies and focusing on quality over quantity, you can make the most of your study hours and achieve significant progress. Here's how to optimize your study time and ensure that every minute counts.

Prioritize Your Study Sessions

Identify the times of day when you are most alert and focused. Schedule your study sessions during these peak periods to maximize productivity. For many people, early morning or late evening hours can be particularly effective. Prioritizing study sessions during these times ensures that you're able to concentrate fully and absorb information more efficiently.

Use the Pomodoro Technique

The Pomodoro Technique is a time management method that involves breaking your study time into focused intervals, typically 25 minutes, followed by a short break. This approach helps maintain high levels of concentration and prevents burnout. Here's how to apply it:

1. **Set a timer** for 25 minutes and focus solely on studying.

2. **Take a 5-minute break** after the timer goes off. Use this time to stretch, hydrate, or relax.

3. **Repeat the cycle** three more times, then take a longer break of 15-30 minutes.

This method not only keeps you engaged but also allows your brain to rest and recharge, improving overall retention and understanding.

| Set a task | Set a timer 25 minutes | Work on the task | Short break 5 minutes | Repeat 4 times | Long break 15 - 30 minutes |

Create a Distraction-Free Environment

Minimize distractions to create a conducive study environment. Find a quiet space where you won't be interrupted, and remove any potential distractions such as your phone, social media, or unnecessary background noise. Consider using apps that block distracting websites or notifications during your study sessions.

Focus on Active Learning

Active learning involves engaging with the material through various techniques rather than passively reading or listening. This approach enhances comprehension and retention. Here are some active learning strategies:

- **Summarize**: After reading a section, summarize the key points in your own words.

- **Question**: Ask yourself questions about the material and try to answer them without looking at your notes.

- **Teach**: Explain the concepts you've learned to someone else, or pretend to teach an imaginary class. Teaching forces you to understand the material thoroughly.

- **Practice**: Complete practice questions and problems related to the topic. Immediate application of knowledge helps reinforce learning.

Leverage Multimedia Resources

Incorporate different types of learning resources to keep your study sessions dynamic and engaging. Use videos, interactive simulations, and online quizzes to complement traditional study methods. Multimedia resources can provide visual and auditory reinforcement, making complex concepts easier to grasp.

Set Specific, Achievable Goals for Each Session

Define clear objectives for each study session to stay focused and motivated. Instead of vague goals like "study math," set specific targets such as "complete 10 algebra practice questions" or "review the rules of grammar." Specific goals give you a clear direction and a sense of accomplishment once achieved.

Take Regular Breaks and Stay Hydrated

Breaks are essential for maintaining high levels of productivity. Follow the Pomodoro Technique or take a 5-10 minute break every hour to stretch, walk around, and refresh your mind. Staying hydrated and maintaining a balanced diet also plays a crucial role in keeping your energy levels up and your mind sharp.

Review and Reflect

At the end of each study session, take a few minutes to review what you've learned and reflect on your progress. This reflection helps consolidate information and identify areas that may need further review. Keeping a study journal where you note down your achievements and any questions that arise can be a helpful practice.

Stay Flexible and Adapt

Be prepared to adjust your study plan as needed. If you find certain techniques or schedules aren't working, don't hesitate to try new approaches. Flexibility is key to finding the most effective study methods for you. Listen to your body and mind, and adapt your plan to ensure that you're studying efficiently and effectively.

By optimizing your study time using these strategies, you'll be able to make significant progress in your GED preparation without feeling overwhelmed. Remember, the goal is not just to study hard but to study smart. Let's move on to explore quick and focused study techniques that will further enhance your learning experience in the next section.

Quick and Focused Study Techniques

Effective GED preparation isn't just about the number of hours you study; it's about how you use those hours. By incorporating quick and focused study techniques into your routine, you can enhance your learning efficiency and retain information better. Here are some of the most effective methods to help you study smart and make the most of your time.

One powerful technique is active recall, which involves testing your memory by retrieving information without looking at your notes. This method strengthens neural connections and improves memory retention. After studying a topic, close your book and try to recall the key points. Write down everything you remember, then check your notes to see what you missed. Practicing active recall regularly will help you retain information more effectively and identify areas that need further review.

Another effective strategy is spaced repetition, which involves reviewing material at increasing intervals. This method leverages the psychological spacing effect, suggesting that information is better retained when reviewed periodically over time. Use flashcards or spaced repetition software to schedule review sessions. Start by reviewing new information within 24 hours, then again after a few days, a week, and so on. This approach reinforces learning and helps transfer knowledge from short-term to long-term memory.

Practice testing is also one of the most effective ways to prepare for the GED. Our online exam simulator provides a realistic testing experience, allowing you to become familiar with the test format and time constraints. After completing each practice test, review your answers thoroughly. Analyze any mistakes to understand where you went wrong and revisit those topics in your study sessions. This continuous cycle of testing and reviewing enhances your test-taking skills and boosts confidence.

In addition to these techniques, creating a distraction-free study environment is crucial for maximizing your productivity. Find a quiet space where you won't be interrupted, and remove any potential distractions such as your phone, social media, or unnecessary background noise. Use apps that block distracting websites or notifications during your study sessions to stay focused.

To reinforce your understanding and evaluate your readiness to implement these study strategies, consider the following checklist:

1. Have I identified the most effective study techniques that work for me, such as active recall, spaced repetition, and practice testing?

2. Am I using the online exam simulator to familiarize myself with the GED test format and timing?

3. Have I created a distraction-free study environment to maximize my focus and productivity?

4. Am I consistently reviewing my practice test results to identify areas that need further improvement?

5. Have I incorporated regular breaks and self-care practices to maintain a positive mindset and avoid burnout?

By prioritizing these essential study techniques and regularly assessing your progress using the checklist, you'll be well on your way to mastering the material and achieving your GED goals. Remember, the key to success is not just working hard but working smart. Embrace these strategies, trust in your abilities, and approach your GED preparation with confidence and determination.

Final Checklist: Assessing Your GED Readiness

Congratulations on completing the strategies and techniques outlined in this chapter! You've taken a significant step towards effective GED preparation. To ensure you're well-equipped to move forward, use this final checklist to evaluate your understanding and readiness:

1. Study Plan:

- Have I created a personalized study plan that fits my schedule and learning style?
- Does my study plan cover all four GED subject areas: Reasoning Through Language Arts, Mathematical Reasoning, Science, and Social Studies?
- Have I allotted sufficient time for each subject, considering my strengths and weaknesses?
- Are my study goals specific, measurable, and achievable?

2. Study Environment:

- Have I designated a quiet, distraction-free space for my study sessions?
- Do I have all the necessary materials, such as books, notes, and practice tests, easily accessible?
- Have I minimized potential distractions, like phone notifications or social media?

3. Study Techniques:

- Am I familiar with the quick and focused study techniques discussed in this chapter, such as active recall, spaced repetition, and practice testing?
- Have I identified the techniques that work best for me and incorporated them into my study routine?
- Am I using the online exam simulator to familiarize myself with the GED test format and timing?
- Do I regularly review my practice test results to identify areas that need further improvement?

4. Time Management:

o   Am I utilizing time management strategies, like the Pomodoro Technique, to maximize my productivity during study sessions?

o   Do I take regular breaks to maintain focus and avoid burnout?

o   Am I consistently tracking my progress and adjusting my study plan as needed?

5. Mindset and Motivation:

o   Do I have a positive and growth-oriented mindset towards my GED preparation?

o   Am I celebrating my small victories and progress along the way?

o   Have I established a support system, whether through family, friends, or a study group, to keep me motivated and accountable?

If you can confidently answer "yes" to most of these questions, you're well-prepared to tackle the GED with the strategies and techniques outlined in this chapter. Remember, preparing for the GED is a journey, and progress is more important than perfection. Continue to refine your study plan, implement the techniques that work best for you, and maintain a positive mindset.

In the following chapters, we'll dive deeper into each of the four GED subject areas, providing you with subject-specific strategies, practice questions, and detailed explanations. By combining the foundational strategies from this chapter with the targeted advice in the upcoming sections, you'll be fully equipped to conquer the GED and achieve your goals.

Keep up the excellent work, stay committed to your study plan, and approach the GED with the confidence that comes from thorough preparation. Your success is within reach, and we're here to support you every step of the way.

CHAPTER 2
7 PROVEN STRATEGIES FOR YOU GED EXAM

Success in the GED test requires more than just understanding the content; it involves mastering effective test-taking strategies that can significantly boost your performance. In this chapter, we'll explore seven proven strategies that will help you tackle the GED exam with confidence and competence. These strategies are designed to optimize your test preparation and ensure you're fully equipped to pass your exam.

Each strategy is grounded in practical advice and backed by research, offering you the tools you need to succeed.

Strategy 1: Understanding the Test Format

Understanding the test format is the first critical step in your preparation. Familiarizing yourself with the structure and types of questions you'll encounter on the GED will help reduce anxiety and improve your efficiency on test day. Here's a detailed breakdown of what you need to know about the test format for each subject area.

Reasoning Through Language Arts (RLA)

The RLA section of the GED test is designed to assess your reading and writing skills. It consists of three main parts:

1. **Reading Comprehension**: You will read a variety of literary and informational texts. Questions will test your ability to understand and interpret these texts, including identifying main ideas, themes, and details.

2. **Writing**: This part includes an extended response (essay) where you must analyze a given argument and write a coherent essay in response. You will be evaluated on your ability to develop a logical argument, use evidence effectively, and write clearly and persuasively.

3. **Grammar and Punctuation**: Questions in this section will test your understanding of standard English conventions, including grammar, punctuation, and sentence structure.

Test Format:

- **Total Duration**: 150 minutes (2 hours and 30 minutes), including a 10-minute break.

- **Question Types**: Multiple-choice, drag-and-drop, drop-down, hot spot, fill-in-the-blank, and extended response (essay).

- **Scoring**: The RLA section is scored on a scale of 100 to 200, with 145 being the passing score.

Mathematical Reasoning

The Mathematical Reasoning section tests your ability to solve mathematical problems using algebraic and quantitative skills. It is divided into two parts:

1. **Part 1**: You are allowed to use a calculator (the TI-30XS MultiView).

2. **Part 2**: Calculator use is not permitted.

Test Format:

- **Total Duration**: 115 minutes (1 hour and 55 minutes).

- **Question Types**: Multiple-choice, drag-and-drop, drop-down, hot spot, fill-in-the-blank.

- **Content Areas**: Algebra (equations, expressions, graphs) and Quantitative Problem Solving (geometry, arithmetic, data analysis).
- **Scoring**: The Mathematical Reasoning section is scored on a scale of 100 to 200, with 145 being the passing score.

Science

The Science section evaluates your understanding of life science, physical science, and earth and space science. It measures your ability to interpret scientific information and apply scientific principles.

Test Format:

- **Total Duration**: 90 minutes (1 hour and 30 minutes).
- **Question Types**: Multiple-choice, drag-and-drop, drop-down, hot spot, fill-in-the-blank, short answer.
- **Content Areas**: Life Science (biology), Physical Science (physics and chemistry), Earth and Space Science.
- **Scoring**: The Science section is scored on a scale of 100 to 200, with 145 being the passing score.

Social Studies

The Social Studies section tests your knowledge of history, geography, civics and government, and economics. It focuses on your ability to analyze and interpret historical texts, data, and maps.

Test Format:

- **Total Duration**: 70 minutes (1 hour and 10 minutes).
- **Question Types**: Multiple-choice, drag-and-drop, drop-down, hot spot, fill-in-the-blank.
- **Content Areas**: U.S. History, World History, Geography, Civics and Government, Economics.
- **Scoring**: The Social Studies section is scored on a scale of 100 to 200, with 145 being the passing score.

Tips for Understanding the Test Format

1. **Familiarize Yourself with Question Types**: Practice with the various types of questions you'll encounter on the test, such as multiple-choice, drag-and-drop, and extended response. This will help you become comfortable with the format and reduce surprises on test day.

2. **Take Full-Length Practice Tests**: Simulate the test environment by taking full-length practice tests under timed conditions. This will help you manage your time effectively and build stamina.

3. **Review the Scoring Criteria**: Understand how each section is scored. Pay special attention to the extended response in the RLA section, as it requires a different approach than multiple-choice questions.

4. **Utilize Official GED Resources**: The official GED website offers sample questions, practice tests, and other resources that are aligned with the actual test format. Make use of these resources to get a realistic sense of what to expect.

5. **Develop Test-Taking Strategies**: Create strategies for answering different types of questions. For example, for multiple-choice questions, eliminate obviously incorrect answers first to increase your chances of selecting the correct one.

By thoroughly understanding the test format, you can approach the GED with confidence and a clear strategy. This foundational knowledge will not only reduce test-day anxiety but also enhance your overall performance. Next, we'll dive into the importance of time management during the test and provide you with practical techniques to make every minute count.

Strategy 2: Time Management During the Test

Effective time management is crucial to succeeding on the GED test. Each section is timed, and managing your time wisely can mean the difference between finishing all the questions or leaving some unanswered. Here's how you can optimize your time during the test and ensure that you complete each section within the allotted time.

Know the Time Limits

Understanding the specific time limits for each section of the GED is the first step in managing your time effectively:

- **Reasoning Through Language Arts (RLA)**: 150 minutes, including a 10-minute break.
- **Mathematical Reasoning**: 115 minutes.
- **Science**: 90 minutes.
- **Social Studies**: 70 minutes.

By being aware of these time constraints, you can plan your pace and avoid spending too much time on any one question or section.

Develop a Timing Strategy

Before the test, practice developing a timing strategy that works for you. Here are some tips to help you manage your time effectively during each section:

1. **Divide Your Time**: Allocate specific amounts of time to different parts of the section. For example, if you have 150 minutes for the RLA section, you might spend 50 minutes on reading comprehension, 40 minutes on writing, and 60 minutes on grammar and the extended response.

2. **Set Milestones**: During your practice tests, set milestones for when you should be halfway through the questions. This helps you gauge whether you're on track and adjust your pace if needed.

3. **Prioritize Questions**: Start with the questions you find easiest. Answering these first can build your confidence and secure easy points. Mark the more challenging questions and return to them later if you have time.

4. **Use the Process of Elimination**: For multiple-choice questions, eliminate obviously incorrect answers first. This increases your chances of choosing the correct answer and saves time.

5. **Pace Yourself**: Don't rush, but also don't spend too much time on a single question. If a question is taking too long, make an educated guess, mark it, and move on. You can always return to it if time permits.

Practice Under Timed Conditions

Simulate the actual test environment by taking practice tests under timed conditions. This will help you get used to the pressure of the clock and develop a natural rhythm for answering questions within the time limits. During these practice sessions, use the following techniques:

- **Timer Practice**: Use a timer to track how long you spend on each question and section. This helps you develop a sense of how much time is passing and whether you need to speed up or slow down.

- **Review Your Performance**: After completing a timed practice test, review your performance to identify areas where you spent too much time. Adjust your timing strategy accordingly.

Stay Calm and Focused

Stress and anxiety can negatively impact your ability to manage time effectively. On test day, it's essential to stay calm and focused:

- **Take Deep Breaths**: If you start to feel overwhelmed, take a few deep breaths to calm yourself. This can help clear your mind and refocus your attention.

- **Stay Positive**: Keep a positive mindset and remind yourself that you've prepared thoroughly. Confidence can improve your efficiency and help you manage your time better.

- **Use Breaks Wisely**: Use any scheduled breaks to relax and recharge. Stretch, hydrate, and give your mind a moment to rest before continuing.

Specific Time Management Tips for Each Section

Reasoning Through Language Arts (RLA)

- **Reading Comprehension**: Spend about 50 minutes. Skim the passages first to get an overview, then read the questions before diving back into the text for detailed reading.

- **Writing**: Allocate around 40 minutes. Spend 10 minutes planning your essay, 25 minutes writing, and 5 minutes reviewing and editing.

- **Grammar and Punctuation**: Use the remaining 60 minutes to answer grammar and punctuation questions, ensuring you leave time for the extended response.

Mathematical Reasoning

- **Calculator Part**: Spend the first 60 minutes here. Use the calculator efficiently and check your work if time allows.

- **Non-Calculator Part**: Use the remaining 55 minutes. Focus on straightforward problems first and come back to more complex ones if time permits.

Science

- **Reading and Interpreting Graphs**: Allocate about 30 minutes. Quickly identify key information and use it to answer questions.

- **Scientific Principles and Concepts**: Spend the remaining 60 minutes here, breaking it down into smaller chunks based on question difficulty.

Social Studies

- **Reading Passages and Analyzing Documents**: Spend around 40 minutes on these tasks. Skim the passages first to get an overview, then read the questions before diving back into the text for detailed reading.

- **Maps and Graphs**: Use the remaining 30 minutes. Identify key information quickly and apply it to answer the questions.

By implementing these time management strategies, you can navigate each section of the GED test efficiently and effectively. Remember, practice makes perfect. The more you practice managing your time, the more comfortable and confident you will become on test day. Let's move on to the next strategy, where we'll delve into critical reading techniques for the RLA section.

Strategy 3: Critical Reading Techniques for RLA

The Reasoning Through Language Arts (RLA) section of the GED test requires strong reading comprehension skills. Critical reading involves more than just understanding the words on the page; it requires analyzing, synthesizing, and evaluating the text to grasp deeper meanings and implications. Here are some critical reading techniques to help you excel in the RLA section.

Active Reading

Active reading means engaging with the text as you read, rather than passively absorbing information. This involves questioning the content, making predictions, and summarizing key points. Here's how to practice active reading:

- **Annotate the Text**: As you read, highlight or underline important information, and jot down notes in the margins. This can include main ideas, key details, and your own thoughts or questions about the text.

- **Ask Questions**: Before, during, and after reading, ask yourself questions about the text. What is the author's purpose? What are the main arguments? How do the details support the main ideas?

- **Make Predictions**: Based on the title, headings, and introductory paragraphs, predict what the text will be about. As you read, adjust your predictions based on new information.

- **Summarize**: After reading a section, pause to summarize the main points in your own words. This helps reinforce your understanding and retention of the material.

Identifying Main Ideas and Supporting Details

One of the key skills in the RLA section is identifying the main ideas and supporting details in a passage. Here's how to hone this skill:

- **Look for Topic Sentences**: The main idea of a paragraph is often found in the topic sentence, which is usually the first or last sentence of the paragraph. Identifying this sentence can help you quickly grasp the main point.

- **Highlight Key Details**: Supporting details provide evidence and examples that reinforce the main idea. Highlight these details as you read to understand how they contribute to the overall argument.

- **Use Organizational Patterns**: Authors often use organizational patterns such as cause and effect, compare and contrast, or problem and solution to structure their ideas. Recognizing these patterns can help you identify main ideas and details more effectively.

Understanding the Author's Purpose and Tone

Recognizing the author's purpose and tone is essential for interpreting the text accurately. Here's how to develop this skill:

- **Determine the Purpose**: Authors write for different purposes, such as to inform, persuade, entertain, or explain. Identifying the purpose helps you understand the context and intent behind the text.

- **Analyze the Tone**: The tone reflects the author's attitude toward the subject. It can be formal, informal, serious, humorous, etc. Pay attention to word choice, sentence structure, and style to discern the tone.

- **Look for Clues**: Phrases that express opinions, emotions, or judgments often reveal the author's purpose and tone. Words like "should," "must," or "unfortunately" can indicate persuasive or emotional intent.

Making Inferences and Drawing Conclusions

The ability to make inferences and draw conclusions from the text is crucial for critical reading. Here's how to practice this skill:

- **Read Between the Lines**: Inferences are logical guesses based on evidence in the text. Pay attention to subtle hints and implied meanings that are not explicitly stated.

- **Connect the Dots**: Use your background knowledge and the information provided in the text to make connections and draw conclusions. Ask yourself what the author is suggesting or implying.

- **Practice with Examples**: Regularly practice making inferences and drawing conclusions with various texts. Start with simpler passages and gradually move to more complex ones.

Evaluating Arguments and Evidence

In the RLA section, you'll need to evaluate the strength of the arguments and the quality of the evidence presented. Here's how to develop this skill:

- **Identify Claims and Evidence**: Determine the main claims or arguments made by the author and the evidence used to support them. Look for facts, statistics, expert opinions, and examples.

- **Assess the Quality**: Evaluate whether the evidence is relevant, reliable, and sufficient to support the claims. Consider the source, context, and credibility of the information.

- **Detect Bias and Assumptions**: Be aware of any biases or assumptions that might influence the author's arguments. Biases can affect the objectivity and fairness of the text.

Practicing with Sample Passages

To apply these critical reading techniques, practice with sample passages similar to those you'll encounter on the GED test. Here's a step-by-step approach:

1. **Read the Passage Thoroughly**: Read the passage carefully, using active reading strategies such as annotating and asking questions.

2. **Identify Key Elements**: Highlight the main ideas, supporting details, and any clues about the author's purpose and tone.

3. **Make Inferences**: Practice making inferences and drawing conclusions based on the information provided.

4. **Evaluate Arguments**: Assess the strength and quality of the arguments and evidence presented.

5. **Answer Practice Questions**: Complete practice questions related to the passage and review the explanations for correct and incorrect answers.

By mastering these critical reading techniques, you'll be better equipped to tackle the RLA section of the GED test with confidence. These skills will not only help you on the test but also enhance your overall reading comprehension and analytical abilities. Next, we'll explore how to approach math problems effectively, ensuring you're prepared for the Mathematical Reasoning section.

Strategy 4: Approaching Math Problems

The Mathematical Reasoning section of the GED test can be challenging, but with the right strategies, you can tackle math problems effectively and confidently. This section tests your ability to apply mathematical concepts to solve real-world problems. Here's how you can approach math problems to maximize your performance.

Understand the Problem

The first step in solving any math problem is understanding what is being asked. Carefully read the problem to identify the key information and what you need to find. Here are some tips to help you understand the problem:

- **Identify Key Information**: Look for numbers, variables, and any specific details that are crucial to solving the problem. Highlight or underline this information.

- **Determine What's Being Asked**: Clearly identify the question you need to answer. Sometimes, the problem might contain extra information that isn't necessary for solving it, so focus on what is relevant.

- **Restate the Problem**: If the problem is complex, try restating it in your own words to ensure you understand it correctly.

Break the Problem Down

Breaking the problem down into smaller, more manageable steps can make it easier to solve. This is especially useful for multi-step problems. Here's how to do it:

- **Simplify the Problem**: If possible, simplify the problem by breaking it into smaller parts. Solve each part step by step.

- **Work Systematically**: Follow a logical sequence of steps to solve the problem. Write down each step to keep track of your work and avoid mistakes.

- **Check Units and Conversions**: Make sure you're using the correct units and perform any necessary conversions before solving the problem.

Use Diagrams and Visuals

Visual aids such as diagrams, graphs, and tables can help you understand and solve math problems more effectively. Here's how to use them:

- **Draw Diagrams**: For geometry problems, drawing a diagram can help you visualize the shapes, angles, and measurements involved.

- **Use Graphs**: For problems involving data, plotting the information on a graph can help you see patterns and relationships more clearly.

- **Create Tables**: For problems that involve organizing data or making comparisons, creating a table can help you organize the information and simplify calculations.

Apply Mathematical Formulas and Concepts

Knowing and applying the right mathematical formulas and concepts is crucial for solving problems efficiently. Here's how to approach this:

- **Memorize Key Formulas**: Make sure you know the key formulas for algebra, geometry, and arithmetic. This includes formulas for area, volume, equations of lines, and basic arithmetic operations.

- **Understand the Concepts**: Beyond memorizing formulas, ensure you understand the underlying concepts. This will help you apply the formulas correctly and adapt them to different types of problems.

- **Practice Regularly**: Regular practice will reinforce your understanding of the formulas and concepts, making it easier to recall and apply them during the test.

Check Your Work

After solving a problem, it's essential to check your work to ensure accuracy. Here's how to review your solution:

- **Revisit Each Step**: Go through each step of your solution to make sure you didn't make any mistakes. Look for common errors such as incorrect arithmetic or misapplied formulas.

- **Verify Units**: Make sure your final answer is in the correct units and that any conversions were done accurately.

- **Use Estimation**: Estimate the answer to see if it's reasonable. If your solution seems off, recheck your calculations.

- **Double-Check Key Calculations**: For critical calculations, double-check your work. This is especially important for complex or multi-step problems.

Practice with a Calculator

The GED test allows the use of a calculator for part of the Mathematical Reasoning section. Here's how to make the most of it:

- **Familiarize Yourself with the Calculator**: Ensure you're comfortable using the TI-30XS MultiView calculator. Practice performing basic and complex calculations to build your proficiency.

- **Know When to Use It**: Use the calculator for calculations that are time-consuming or prone to error, but also practice doing some calculations manually to keep your skills sharp.

- **Check Calculator Entries**: Always double-check your entries to avoid mistakes. A small error in input can lead to an incorrect answer.

Apply Problem-Solving Strategies

Using effective problem-solving strategies can help you tackle a wide range of math problems. Here are some strategies to consider:

- **Work Backwards**: For some problems, starting with the answer and working backwards can help you understand the steps needed to solve it.

- **Look for Patterns**: Identify patterns in the problem that can help you find a solution. This is especially useful for algebra and geometry problems.

- **Use Logical Reasoning**: Apply logical reasoning to eliminate incorrect answers and narrow down your choices. This is helpful for multiple-choice questions.

Practice, Practice, Practice

Consistent practice is key to mastering math problems. Here's how to make the most of your practice sessions:

- **Use Practice Questions**: Regularly solve practice questions that cover a variety of math topics. This will help you become familiar with different types of problems and improve your problem-solving skills.

- **Take Practice Tests**: Simulate the test environment by taking full-length practice tests under timed conditions. This will help you manage your time and build confidence.

- **Review Mistakes**: Analyze any mistakes you make during practice. Understand why you got a question wrong and learn from it to avoid repeating the same errors.

By implementing these strategies, you can approach math problems with confidence and efficiency. Remember, the key to success in math is understanding the concepts, practicing regularly, and applying effective problem-solving techniques. Let's move on to the next strategy, where we'll explore scientific interpretation skills to help you excel in the Science section of the GED test.

Strategy 5: Scientific Interpretation Skills

The Science section of the GED test requires not only a basic understanding of scientific concepts but also the ability to interpret and analyze scientific information. This includes reading and understanding graphs, tables, and diagrams, as well as drawing conclusions from experimental data. Here are some strategies to enhance your scientific interpretation skills and excel in this section.

Understand Scientific Concepts

A solid grasp of fundamental scientific concepts is essential. The GED Science section covers three main areas: Life Science, Physical Science, and Earth and Space Science. Here's how to build a strong foundation:

- **Review Basic Principles**: Make sure you understand the key concepts in biology, chemistry, physics, and earth science. Focus on topics such as cell biology, genetics, ecosystems, chemical reactions, forces, energy, and the structure of the Earth and the solar system.

- **Use Reliable Resources**: Utilize textbooks, educational websites, and online courses to review and reinforce your knowledge. The explanations in this book will also help clarify complex topics.

- **Summarize Key Points**: After studying each topic, summarize the main points in your own words. This helps reinforce your understanding and makes it easier to recall information during the test.

Interpret Graphs and Tables

Graphs and tables are common in the Science section, and being able to interpret them accurately is crucial. Here's how to approach these data presentations:

- **Identify the Type of Graph or Table**: Understand the different types of graphs (e.g., bar graphs, line graphs, pie charts) and tables. Each type presents data in a specific way, and recognizing the format helps you interpret the information correctly.

- **Read the Labels**: Pay close attention to the labels on the axes of graphs and the headings of tables. These labels tell you what data is being presented and how to read it.

- **Analyze Trends and Patterns**: Look for trends, patterns, and relationships in the data. For example, in a line graph, observe how the data points change over time or with different conditions.

- **Draw Conclusions**: Based on the data presented, make logical conclusions. Ask yourself what the data indicates and how it supports or refutes a hypothesis.

Understand Scientific Experiments

Many questions in the Science section involve understanding and analyzing scientific experiments. Here's how to approach these questions:

- **Identify the Hypothesis**: Determine the hypothesis or research question that the experiment is designed to test. Understanding the purpose of the experiment helps you interpret the results.

- **Understand the Variables**: Identify the independent variable (what is being changed) and the dependent variable (what is being measured). Also, consider any control variables that are kept constant to ensure a fair test.

- **Analyze the Results**: Look at the data or results of the experiment. Consider how the independent variable affected the dependent variable and whether the results support the hypothesis.

- **Evaluate the Experimental Design**: Assess the strengths and weaknesses of the experimental design. Consider whether there are any sources of error or bias that could affect the results.

Use the Scientific Method

The scientific method is a systematic approach to solving problems and answering questions. Here's how to apply it:

1. **Ask a Question**: Start with a clear, specific question that you want to answer.

2. **Conduct Background Research**: Gather information and resources to understand the context of the question.

3. **Form a Hypothesis**: Make an educated guess or prediction that can be tested.

4. **Conduct an Experiment**: Design and perform an experiment to test the hypothesis. Collect and record data.

5. **Analyze the Data**: Review the data to determine whether it supports or refutes the hypothesis.

6. **Draw Conclusions**: Based on the data analysis, draw conclusions and consider whether the hypothesis was correct.

7. **Communicate Results**: Share the findings with others. This could involve writing a report or presenting the results.

Practice Critical Thinking

Critical thinking is essential for interpreting scientific information. Here's how to develop this skill:

- **Ask Questions**: Always ask questions about the information presented. Why is this important? What evidence supports this claim? What are the implications?

- **Evaluate Sources**: Consider the reliability and credibility of the sources of scientific information. Peer-reviewed journals, reputable organizations, and educational institutions are typically reliable sources.

- **Consider Alternative Explanations**: Think about other possible explanations for the data or results. This helps you evaluate the strength of the conclusions.

Apply Scientific Interpretation Skills

To apply these skills, practice with a variety of scientific texts and data presentations. Here's a step-by-step approach:

1. **Read Scientific Passages**: Read passages that describe scientific concepts, experiments, and data. Practice interpreting the information and answering related questions.

2. **Analyze Graphs and Tables**: Work with different types of graphs and tables. Practice identifying trends, drawing conclusions, and making inferences based on the data.

3. **Evaluate Experiments**: Review descriptions of scientific experiments. Practice identifying the hypothesis, variables, and analyzing the results.

4. **Answer Practice Questions**: Complete practice questions that involve scientific interpretation. Review the explanations for correct and incorrect answers to understand your mistakes and improve your skills.

By mastering these scientific interpretation skills, you'll be well-prepared to tackle the Science section of the GED test. These skills not only help you understand and analyze scientific information but also enhance your overall critical thinking abilities. Let's move on to the next strategy, where we'll explore how to analyze data and graphs in the Social Studies section.

Strategy 6: Analyzing Data and Graphs in Social Studies

The Social Studies section of the GED test not only assesses your knowledge of history, geography, civics, and economics but also your ability to analyze and interpret data presented in various forms, such as graphs, tables, and charts. Developing strong skills in data analysis is crucial for understanding trends, drawing conclusions, and making informed decisions based on historical and social data. Here are some strategies to help you excel in analyzing data and graphs in the Social Studies section.

Understand Different Types of Data Presentations

Graphs, tables, and charts are commonly used to present data in the Social Studies section. Here's a brief overview of the different types you might encounter and how to approach them:

- **Bar Graphs**: Bar graphs are used to compare quantities across different categories. Pay attention to the labels on the x-axis (categories) and y-axis (values). Compare the heights of the bars to determine which categories have higher or lower values.

- **Line Graphs**: Line graphs display data points connected by lines, often showing trends over time. Look at the x-axis (usually time) and y-axis (values) to understand the trend. Notice whether the line is increasing, decreasing, or remaining constant.

- **Pie Charts**: Pie charts show the proportions of a whole, divided into slices. Each slice represents a percentage of the total. Compare the sizes of the slices to understand the relative proportions.

- **Tables**: Tables organize data into rows and columns, making it easy to compare information. Read the headings carefully to understand what each row and column represents.

- **Maps**: Maps may include data such as population density, economic activity, or political boundaries. Pay attention to the legend and scale to interpret the map accurately.

Read the Data Carefully

Careful reading and interpretation of data are essential. Here's how to approach it:

- **Examine the Titles and Labels**: The title of the graph, table, or chart provides a summary of what the data represents. Labels on the axes or columns give specific details about the data.

- **Check the Units of Measurement**: Ensure you understand the units used in the data (e.g., percentages, millions, dollars). This helps in making accurate comparisons and calculations.

- **Analyze the Source**: Sometimes, understanding the source of the data can provide context that helps in interpretation. Reliable sources increase the credibility of the data.

Identify Trends and Patterns

Recognizing trends and patterns in data is a key skill. Here's how to do it:

- **Look for Trends**: In line graphs, identify whether the trend is upward, downward, or static. In bar graphs and pie charts, compare the values to see which categories or slices are the largest or smallest.

- **Spot Patterns**: Look for recurring patterns or anomalies in the data. For example, in a table showing population growth over several decades, note any periods of rapid increase or decrease.

- **Make Comparisons**: Use the data to compare different groups, time periods, or geographical areas. Ask yourself what the comparisons reveal about the subject being studied.

Draw Conclusions from the Data

Using the data to draw informed conclusions is essential for the Social Studies section. Here's how to practice this skill:

- **Make Inferences**: Based on the data, make logical inferences about what it indicates. For example, if a line graph shows a steady increase in unemployment rates, infer the possible causes and implications of this trend.

- **Evaluate Implications**: Consider the broader implications of the data. For example, what does a pie chart showing the distribution of government spending reveal about national priorities?

- **Support Your Conclusions**: Use specific data points to support your conclusions. Reference the exact figures or trends that led you to your inference.

Practice with Sample Data

To improve your data analysis skills, practice with a variety of sample graphs, tables, and charts. Here's a step-by-step approach:

1. **Read the Data Presentation**: Carefully examine the graph, table, or chart. Note the title, labels, units, and source.

2. **Identify Key Points**: Highlight or jot down the key points, such as major trends, highest or lowest values, and significant patterns.

3. **Draw Conclusions**: Based on your analysis, draw conclusions and make inferences. Practice writing brief explanations of what the data indicates.

4. **Answer Practice Questions**: Complete practice questions related to the data. Review the explanations for correct and incorrect answers to understand your mistakes and improve your skills.

Apply Data Analysis to Real-World Scenarios

Applying data analysis skills to real-world scenarios enhances your understanding and prepares you for the test. Here's how to do it:

- **Current Events**: Analyze data from current events, such as election results, economic reports, or social surveys. Practice interpreting this data and drawing conclusions.

- **Historical Data**: Review historical data, such as population growth, economic trends, or social changes. Analyze how these trends have shaped current events and societal structures.

- **Geographical Data**: Use maps and geographic data to understand demographic patterns, natural resources, or economic activities. Practice interpreting these maps and making inferences.

By mastering the skills of analyzing data and graphs, you'll be well-prepared to tackle the Social Studies section of the GED test. These skills will not only help you succeed on the test but also enhance your ability to interpret and understand complex information in everyday life. Let's move on to the next strategy, where we'll discuss how to overcome test anxiety and perform at your best on test day.

Strategy 7: Overcoming Test Anxiety

Test anxiety can be a significant barrier to performing well on the GED test. It can cause stress, distract your focus, and negatively impact your ability to recall information and think clearly. However, with the right strategies, you can manage and overcome test anxiety, ensuring you perform at your best on test day. Here's how to tackle test anxiety effectively.

Understand Test Anxiety

Test anxiety is a psychological condition that involves extreme stress, fear, and worry before or during a test. It can manifest in various ways, including physical symptoms (like a racing heart or sweating), emotional symptoms (like feelings of dread or panic), and cognitive symptoms (like difficulty concentrating or negative thinking). Understanding that test anxiety is common and manageable is the first step toward overcoming it.

Preparation is Key

One of the most effective ways to combat test anxiety is thorough preparation. The more prepared you are, the more confident you'll feel. Here's how to prepare effectively:

- **Consistent Study Routine**: Establish a consistent study routine well in advance of the test date. Regular study sessions help you retain information better and reduce last-minute cramming.

- **Practice Tests**: Take full-length practice tests under timed conditions. Familiarizing yourself with the test format and timing can reduce anxiety and improve your test-taking skills.

- **Review and Revise**: Regularly review and revise key concepts. Use flashcards, summaries, and practice questions to reinforce your learning.

Develop Relaxation Techniques

Incorporating relaxation techniques into your routine can help manage anxiety. Here are some effective techniques to try:

- **Deep Breathing**: Practice deep breathing exercises to calm your nervous system. Breathe in slowly through your nose, hold for a few seconds, and then exhale slowly through your mouth. Repeat this several times to reduce stress.

- **Progressive Muscle Relaxation**: This technique involves tensing and then slowly relaxing each muscle group in your body. Start with your toes and work your way up to your head. This can help release physical tension.

- **Visualization**: Visualize yourself succeeding on the test. Imagine walking into the test center feeling confident and calm, answering questions with ease, and receiving a passing score. Positive visualization can boost your confidence and reduce anxiety.

Stay Positive and Challenge Negative Thoughts

Negative thoughts can exacerbate test anxiety. Learning to challenge and replace these thoughts with positive ones can make a big difference. Here's how:

- **Identify Negative Thoughts**: Pay attention to any negative thoughts that arise, such as "I'm going to fail" or "I'm not good at this."

- **Challenge These Thoughts**: Ask yourself whether these thoughts are rational and based on evidence. Often, negative thoughts are exaggerated and unrealistic.

- **Replace with Positive Affirmations**: Replace negative thoughts with positive affirmations. For example, "I have prepared well for this test" or "I am capable of doing this." Repeat these affirmations to yourself regularly.

Develop a Test-Day Plan

Having a plan for test day can help reduce anxiety and ensure you're prepared. Here's what to include in your test-day plan:

- **Get a Good Night's Sleep**: Ensure you get plenty of rest the night before the test. A well-rested mind performs better.

- **Eat a Healthy Breakfast**: Eat a nutritious breakfast on the morning of the test to fuel your brain and maintain energy levels.

- **Arrive Early**: Plan to arrive at the test center early to avoid any last-minute stress. This gives you time to settle in and get comfortable.

- **Bring Necessary Materials**: Ensure you have all the necessary materials, such as your ID, admission ticket, and any allowed resources like a calculator.

During the Test

Managing anxiety during the test is crucial for maintaining focus and performing well. Here's how to stay calm and focused:

- **Pace Yourself**: Keep an eye on the time, but don't rush. Pace yourself to ensure you have enough time to answer all the questions.

- **Take Short Breaks**: If allowed, take short breaks to stretch and relax. Even a brief pause can help reset your mind and reduce anxiety.

- **Stay Focused on the Present**: Concentrate on the question at hand rather than worrying about previous or upcoming questions. Taking one question at a time can help maintain focus.

- **Use Relaxation Techniques**: If you start feeling anxious, use deep breathing or visualization techniques to calm yourself.

Practice Self-Care

Taking care of your overall well-being can significantly impact your ability to manage test anxiety. Here are some self-care practices to incorporate:

- **Regular Exercise**: Physical activity can reduce stress and improve mood. Incorporate regular exercise into your routine.

- **Healthy Diet**: Eating a balanced diet can improve your overall health and energy levels.

- **Adequate Sleep**: Ensure you get enough sleep each night to support cognitive function and emotional well-being.

- **Mindfulness and Meditation**: Practice mindfulness or meditation to enhance your ability to stay present and reduce anxiety.

By implementing these strategies, you can effectively manage and overcome test anxiety, allowing you to perform at your best on test day. Remember, anxiety is a normal part of the test-taking process, but with preparation, relaxation techniques, and a positive mindset, you can keep it under control. Now that you've equipped yourself with these essential strategies, you're ready to tackle the GED test with confidence and determination.

CHAPTER 3
REASONING THROUGH LANGUAGE ARTS (RLA)

The Reasoning Through Language Arts (RLA) section of the GED test is designed to assess your reading comprehension, writing, and grammar skills. It evaluates your ability to understand and analyze written texts, construct coherent and well-structured essays, and apply standard English conventions in writing. This chapter will guide you through each component of the RLA section, providing you with the skills and strategies needed to excel. From reading and interpreting complex texts to mastering grammar and punctuation, you'll find comprehensive coverage and practical tips to enhance your performance.

Section Overview

The RLA section of the GED test is divided into three main components: Reading Skills, Writing and Text Structure, and Grammar and Punctuation. Each component plays a crucial role in evaluating your overall language arts proficiency. Here's a detailed overview of what to expect in this section:

Test Structure and Timing

The RLA section is 150 minutes long, including a 10-minute break. It consists of a variety of question types, including multiple-choice, drag-and-drop, drop-down, hot spot, and extended response (essay). Here's a breakdown of the test structure:

- **Reading Comprehension**: This part assesses your ability to read and understand literary and informational texts. You'll encounter passages from various genres and be asked questions that test your comprehension, analysis, and interpretation skills.

- **Writing and Text Structure**: This component evaluates your ability to write effectively and understand the structure of different types of texts. You'll need to analyze how authors develop their arguments and how different elements of a text contribute to its overall meaning.

- **Grammar and Punctuation**: This section tests your knowledge of standard English conventions, including grammar, punctuation, sentence structure, and usage. You'll be required to identify and correct errors in written passages.

- **Extended Response (Essay)**: The essay section requires you to write a coherent and well-structured essay in response to a given prompt. You'll need to develop an argument, support it with evidence, and demonstrate clear and effective writing.

Scoring

Each component of the RLA section contributes to your overall score, which ranges from 100 to 200. A score of 145 is required to pass. The essay is scored separately by trained evaluators who assess your writing based on specific criteria, including organization, clarity, and use of evidence.

Skills Assessed

The RLA section assesses a range of skills critical for success in both academic and professional settings. These skills include:

- **Reading Comprehension**: The ability to understand, analyze, and interpret written texts.

- **Critical Thinking**: The capacity to evaluate arguments, identify biases, and draw logical conclusions.

- **Writing**: The skill to construct clear, coherent, and well-structured written responses.

- **Grammar and Usage**: The knowledge of standard English conventions, including grammar, punctuation, and sentence structure.

Preparation Tips

To excel in the RLA section, it's important to develop a well-rounded approach to studying. Here are some tips to help you prepare effectively:

- **Practice Reading**: Read a variety of texts, including fiction, non-fiction, essays, and articles. Practice summarizing the main ideas and analyzing the author's purpose and techniques.

- **Enhance Writing Skills**: Practice writing essays on various topics. Focus on developing clear arguments, supporting them with evidence, and organizing your writing logically.

- **Review Grammar Rules**: Study standard English conventions, including grammar, punctuation, and sentence structure. Complete practice exercises to reinforce your understanding.

- **Take Practice Tests**: Familiarize yourself with the test format by taking full-length practice tests. This will help you manage your time effectively and build confidence.

By understanding the structure and expectations of the RLA section, you can approach your preparation with confidence and clarity. Let's dive deeper into each component, starting with Reading Skills.

Reading Skills

Reading comprehension is a fundamental aspect of the RLA section. This component evaluates your ability to read and understand complex texts, ranging from literary works to informational articles. Here's how to develop and enhance your reading skills:

Types of Texts

In the RLA section, you'll encounter a variety of texts, including:

- **Literary Texts**: These include fiction, poetry, and drama. Literary texts often focus on themes, character development, and stylistic elements.

- **Informational Texts**: These include non-fiction works, such as essays, articles, and reports. Informational texts focus on presenting facts, arguments, and explanations.

Reading Strategies

To effectively understand and analyze these texts, apply the following reading strategies:

- **Preview the Text**: Before diving into the details, quickly skim the text to get an overview. Look at the title, headings, and any highlighted or bolded sections.

- **Active Reading**: Engage with the text by highlighting key points, annotating in the margins, and asking questions as you read. This helps maintain focus and enhances comprehension.

- **Identify Main Ideas**: Determine the main ideas or arguments presented in the text. Look for topic sentences in paragraphs and summary statements.

- **Analyze Structure**: Understand how the text is organized. Identify the introduction, body, and conclusion, and analyze how each part contributes to the overall meaning.

- **Evaluate Evidence**: Assess the evidence used to support arguments. Determine whether the evidence is relevant, reliable, and sufficient.

- **Infer Meaning**: Make inferences based on the information provided. Look for implied meanings and draw logical conclusions.

Practice Exercises

To improve your reading skills, regularly practice with a variety of texts. Here are some exercises to try:

- **Summarize Texts**: After reading a passage, write a brief summary of the main points. This helps reinforce your understanding and recall.

- **Analyze Arguments**: Identify the arguments presented in an article and evaluate the evidence used to support them. Practice identifying biases and logical fallacies.

- **Answer Comprehension Questions**: Complete practice questions that test your understanding of the text. Review the explanations for correct and incorrect answers to learn from your mistakes.

Reading Skills

Reading comprehension is a critical component of the Reasoning Through Language Arts (RLA) section. It tests your ability to understand, interpret, and analyze various types of texts. To excel in this section, you need to develop a range of reading skills that will help you navigate complex passages and answer questions accurately. This section will guide you through the essential reading skills needed for the GED test, providing strategies and practice exercises to enhance your comprehension abilities.

Types of Texts

The RLA section includes a variety of texts, each requiring a different approach for comprehension and analysis:

- **Literary Texts**: These include works of fiction, poetry, and drama. Literary texts often explore themes, character development, and stylistic elements. Understanding literary devices, such as metaphor, simile, and symbolism, is crucial for analyzing these texts.

- **Informational Texts**: These are non-fiction works such as essays, articles, reports, and manuals. Informational texts present facts, arguments, and explanations. Key skills include identifying main ideas, supporting details, and the structure of the text.

Key Reading Strategies

To effectively understand and analyze texts, apply the following reading strategies:

Preview the Text

Before diving into the details, take a moment to preview the text. This involves quickly skimming the passage to get a sense of its structure and content. Look at the title, headings, subheadings, and any highlighted or bolded sections. This initial overview helps set the context and prepares you for more detailed reading.

Active Reading

Active reading involves engaging with the text rather than passively consuming it. Here's how to practice active reading:

- **Annotate the Text**: Highlight or underline key points, and jot down notes in the margins. Mark important ideas, arguments, and evidence. This keeps you focused and helps reinforce understanding.

- **Ask Questions**: As you read, ask yourself questions about the text. What is the author's purpose? What are the main arguments? How do the details support the main ideas? Asking questions encourages critical thinking and deeper engagement with the text.

- **Summarize Sections**: After reading a section or paragraph, pause to summarize the main points in your own words. This reinforces comprehension and helps retain information.

Identify Main Ideas and Supporting Details

One of the most important skills in reading comprehension is identifying the main ideas and supporting details. Here's how to practice this skill:

- **Find Topic Sentences**: The main idea of a paragraph is often found in the topic sentence, typically the first or last sentence of the paragraph. Identifying the topic sentence helps you quickly grasp the central point.

- **Highlight Key Details**: Supporting details provide evidence and examples that reinforce the main idea. Highlight or underline these details as you read to understand how they contribute to the overall argument.

- **Summarize Main Ideas**: After reading a passage, write a brief summary of the main ideas and supporting details. This helps reinforce your understanding and recall.

Analyze Text Structure

Understanding the structure of a text helps you see how the author organizes and presents information. Here's how to analyze text structure:

- **Identify Organizational Patterns**: Authors often use specific organizational patterns, such as cause and effect, compare and contrast, problem and solution, or chronological order. Recognizing these patterns helps you follow the author's logic and structure.

- **Analyze Paragraph Structure**: Within paragraphs, look at how sentences are organized to support the main idea. Identify the introduction, supporting details, and conclusion.

- **Evaluate Transitions**: Notice how the author uses transition words and phrases to connect ideas and guide the reader through the text. Understanding these transitions helps you follow the flow of the argument.

Evaluate Arguments and Evidence

Critical reading involves evaluating the strength and validity of the arguments and evidence presented. Here's how to develop this skill:

- **Identify Claims**: Determine the main claims or arguments made by the author. Look for statements that express the author's main points or conclusions.

- **Assess Evidence**: Evaluate the evidence used to support the claims. Consider whether the evidence is relevant, reliable, and sufficient. Look for facts, statistics, expert opinions, and examples.

- **Detect Bias and Assumptions**: Be aware of any biases or assumptions that might influence the author's arguments. Consider how these biases might affect the objectivity and credibility of the text.

Make Inferences and Draw Conclusions

Making inferences and drawing conclusions from the text is a key reading skill. Here's how to practice this:

- **Read Between the Lines**: Inferences are logical guesses based on evidence in the text. Pay attention to subtle hints and implied meanings that are not explicitly stated.

- **Connect the Dots**: Use your background knowledge and the information provided in the text to make connections and draw conclusions. Ask yourself what the author is suggesting or implying.

- **Practice with Examples**: Regularly practice making inferences and drawing conclusions with various texts. Start with simpler passages and gradually move to more complex ones.

Practice Exercises

To enhance your reading skills, practice regularly with a variety of texts. Here are some exercises to try:

- **Summarize Passages**: After reading a passage, write a brief summary of the main points. This helps reinforce your understanding and recall.

- **Analyze Arguments**: Identify the arguments presented in an article and evaluate the evidence used to support them. Practice identifying biases and logical fallacies.

- **Answer Comprehension Questions**: Complete practice questions that test your understanding of the text. Review the explanations for correct and incorrect answers to learn from your mistakes.

By developing these reading skills, you'll be well-prepared to tackle the reading comprehension component of the RLA section. These skills will not only help you on the GED test but also enhance your overall ability to understand and analyze written texts. Next, we'll explore Writing and Text Structure, where you'll learn how to construct clear and coherent written responses and analyze the structure of different types of texts.

Writing and Text Structure

Writing effectively and understanding the structure of various texts are crucial skills for the Reasoning Through Language Arts (RLA) section of the GED test. This component evaluates your ability to construct coherent, well-organized essays and analyze the organizational elements of written works. In this section, we will explore essential writing strategies and provide specific tools to help you excel.

Understanding Text Structure

Different types of texts follow various organizational patterns. Recognizing these patterns helps you comprehend and analyze texts more effectively. Here are some common text structures:

Narrative Structure

- **Definition**: Narrative texts tell a story, typically with a clear beginning, middle, and end.
- **Elements**: Look for elements like setting, characters, plot, conflict, and resolution.
- **Purpose**: The purpose is often to entertain or inform through storytelling.

Expository Structure

- **Definition**: Expository texts explain, describe, or inform.
- **Elements**: These include an introduction, body paragraphs with supporting details, and a conclusion.
- **Purpose**: The purpose is to provide information or explain a topic clearly.

Persuasive Structure

- **Definition**: Persuasive texts aim to convince the reader of a particular viewpoint.
- **Elements**: These include a clear thesis, supporting arguments, evidence, and a conclusion that reinforces the main argument.
- **Purpose**: The purpose is to persuade the reader to adopt a certain perspective or take action.

Descriptive Structure

- **Definition**: Descriptive texts provide detailed descriptions of a subject.
- **Elements**: These include sensory details that appeal to the senses (sight, sound, smell, touch, taste).
- **Purpose**: The purpose is to paint a vivid picture of the subject for the reader.

Writing Effective Essays

Writing well-structured essays is a critical skill for the RLA section. Here are some steps and tools to help you craft effective essays:

Step 1: Understand the Prompt

- **Read Carefully**: Carefully read the essay prompt to understand what is being asked. Identify the key question or task.

- **Underline Keywords**: Highlight important keywords in the prompt that indicate the focus of your essay.

Step 2: Plan Your Essay

- **Brainstorm Ideas**: Take a few minutes to brainstorm ideas related to the prompt. Jot down any thoughts or arguments that come to mind.

- **Organize Your Thoughts**: Arrange your ideas into a logical order. Decide on the main points you want to cover and the order in which to present them.

- **Create an Outline**: Develop a basic outline that includes an introduction, body paragraphs, and a conclusion. This helps organize your essay and ensures a clear flow of ideas.

Step 3: Write the Introduction

- **Hook the Reader**: Start with a hook that grabs the reader's attention. This could be a quote, a question, or a surprising fact.

- **Introduce the Topic**: Provide some background information on the topic to set the context.

- **State the Thesis**: Clearly state your thesis or main argument. This serves as the central point of your essay.

Step 4: Develop Body Paragraphs

- **Topic Sentences**: Begin each paragraph with a topic sentence that introduces the main idea of the paragraph.

- **Provide Evidence**: Support your arguments with evidence, such as facts, examples, or quotes. Make sure the evidence is relevant and strengthens your argument.

- **Analyze and Explain**: Explain how the evidence supports your thesis. Analyze the significance of the evidence and connect it to your main argument.

- **Use Transitions**: Use transition words and phrases to connect ideas between paragraphs and maintain a smooth flow.

Step 5: Write the Conclusion

- **Summarize Main Points**: Briefly summarize the main points discussed in the body paragraphs.

- **Restate the Thesis**: Reinforce your thesis statement, but don't simply repeat it word for word.

- **Leave a Lasting Impression**: End with a final thought or call to action that leaves a lasting impression on the reader.

Tools for Effective Writing

To help you write more effectively, here are some specific tools and techniques:

Graphic Organizers

- **Definition**: Graphic organizers are visual tools that help organize information.
- **Types**: These include Venn diagrams, mind maps, and T-charts.
- **Use**: Use graphic organizers to brainstorm ideas, organize thoughts, and outline your essay.

Writing Templates

- **Definition**: Writing templates provide a structured format for writing essays.
- **Types**: These can include templates for introductory paragraphs, body paragraphs, and conclusions.
- **Use**: Use writing templates to ensure your essay follows a clear and logical structure.

Sentence Starters

- **Definition**: Sentence starters are phrases that help begin sentences and paragraphs.
- **Examples**: "For instance…," "In addition…," "Therefore…," "As a result…"
- **Use**: Use sentence starters to create smooth transitions and enhance the flow of your writing.

Editing and Revising Techniques

- **Self-Review**: After writing your essay, take a break and then review it with fresh eyes. Look for any errors or areas that need improvement.
- **Peer Review**: Ask a friend or family member to review your essay. They can provide valuable feedback and catch mistakes you might have missed.
- **Checklists**: Use a checklist to ensure you've included all necessary components in your essay, such as a clear thesis, supporting evidence, and proper grammar.

Practice Exercises

To improve your writing skills, practice regularly. Here are some exercises to try:

- **Write Regularly**: Set aside time each day or week to write essays on various topics. Practice makes perfect.
- **Peer Review Sessions**: Join a study group or partner with a friend to review each other's essays and provide constructive feedback.

- **Use Writing Prompts**: Use GED practice prompts to simulate the test environment. Write essays based on these prompts and review them using the tools and techniques mentioned above.

By developing strong writing skills and understanding text structure, you'll be well-prepared to tackle the writing component of the RLA section. These skills will not only help you succeed on the GED test but also enhance your overall ability to communicate effectively through writing. Next, we'll explore Grammar and Punctuation, where you'll learn how to apply standard English conventions accurately in your writing.

Grammar and Punctuation

Grammar and punctuation are fundamental components of effective writing. Mastery of these elements not only enhances the clarity and coherence of your writing but also ensures that your ideas are conveyed accurately and professionally. In the Reasoning Through Language Arts (RLA) section of the GED test, you will be evaluated on your ability to use standard English conventions correctly. This section provides an in-depth look at essential grammar and punctuation rules, along with practical tools and exercises to help you improve your skills.

Understanding Grammar

Grammar involves the rules and structures that govern the composition of sentences. Here are some key grammatical concepts to master:

Parts of Speech

- **Nouns**: Words that name people, places, things, or ideas (e.g., cat, city, happiness).
- **Pronouns**: Words that replace nouns (e.g., he, she, they, it).
- **Verbs**: Words that express actions or states of being (e.g., run, is, seem).
- **Adjectives**: Words that describe nouns or pronouns (e.g., blue, tall, quick).
- **Adverbs**: Words that describe verbs, adjectives, or other adverbs (e.g., quickly, very, well).
- **Prepositions**: Words that show relationships between nouns or pronouns and other words in a sentence (e.g., in, on, at).
- **Conjunctions**: Words that connect words, phrases, or clauses (e.g., and, but, or).
- **Interjections**: Words that express strong emotions (e.g., oh, wow, ouch).

Sentence Structure

- **Simple Sentences**: Contain one independent clause (e.g., The cat sleeps.).
- **Compound Sentences**: Contain two or more independent clauses joined by a conjunction or semicolon (e.g., The cat sleeps, and the dog barks.).
- **Complex Sentences**: Contain one independent clause and one or more dependent clauses (e.g., The cat sleeps when the house is quiet.).
- **Compound-Complex Sentences**: Contain two or more independent clauses and one or more dependent clauses (e.g., The cat sleeps when the house is quiet, and the dog barks.).

Agreement

- **Subject-Verb Agreement**: Ensure that subjects and verbs agree in number (e.g., She runs. They run.).

- **Pronoun-Antecedent Agreement**: Ensure that pronouns agree with their antecedents in number and gender (e.g., The boy lost his book.).

Verb Tenses

- **Past**: Actions that have already happened (e.g., walked).

- **Present**: Actions that are currently happening or general truths (e.g., walk/walks).

- **Future**: Actions that will happen (e.g., will walk).

Modifiers

- **Adjectives and Adverbs**: Place modifiers close to the words they modify to avoid confusion (e.g., She quickly ran. vs. She ran quickly.).

Mastering Punctuation

Punctuation marks are symbols that help organize and clarify written language. Here are some essential punctuation rules:

Periods (.)

- **End of Sentences**: Use a period to mark the end of a declarative sentence (e.g., She went to the store.).

- **Abbreviations**: Use periods in abbreviations (e.g., Dr., Mr., U.S.).

Commas (,)

- **Lists**: Separate items in a list (e.g., apples, oranges, and bananas).

- **Compound Sentences**: Place before a conjunction in a compound sentence (e.g., I wanted to go, but it was raining.).

- **Introductory Elements**: Set off introductory words, phrases, or clauses (e.g., After the game, we went home.).

- **Nonessential Information**: Set off nonessential clauses or phrases (e.g., The car, which was red, sped away.).

Semicolons (;)

- **Independent Clauses**: Connect closely related independent clauses (e.g., I have a big test tomorrow; I can't go out tonight.).

- **Complex Lists**: Separate items in a list when the items contain commas (e.g., The meeting included John, the manager; Sarah, the assistant; and Paul, the consultant.).

Colons (:)

- **Introductions**: Introduce a list, quotation, or explanation (e.g., She brought many items: a pen, a notebook, and a calculator.).

- **Emphasis**: Emphasize a point (e.g., There was one thing she loved most: chocolate.).

Quotation Marks (" ")

- **Direct Speech**: Enclose direct speech or quotations (e.g., She said, "I'm coming over.").

- **Titles**: Enclose titles of short works (e.g., "The Tell-Tale Heart").

Apostrophes (')

- **Possession**: Show possession (e.g., Sarah's book).

- **Contractions**: Indicate omitted letters in contractions (e.g., don't, it's).

Practical Tools for Grammar and Punctuation

To improve your grammar and punctuation skills, use the following tools and techniques:

Grammar Checkers

- **Software**: Use grammar checking software like Grammarly or the built-in tools in word processors. These tools can help identify and correct errors in real-time.

Reference Books

- **Style Guides**: Refer to style guides such as "The Elements of Style" by Strunk and White for detailed rules and examples.

Practice Exercises

- **Workbooks**: Use grammar and punctuation workbooks to practice specific skills. Complete exercises and review the explanations for correct answers.

- **Online Resources**: Utilize online resources like Purdue OWL for comprehensive guides and interactive exercises.

Writing and Revision

- **Drafting**: Write drafts of essays and review them for grammatical and punctuation errors. Focus on one type of error at a time (e.g., first check for subject-verb agreement, then for comma usage).

- **Peer Review**: Exchange essays with a peer and review each other's work. This provides a fresh perspective and helps identify errors you might have missed.

Practice Exercises

To solidify your understanding of grammar and punctuation, engage in regular practice. Here are some exercises to try:

Sentence Correction

- **Identify Errors**: Review sentences and identify grammatical or punctuation errors. Correct the errors and explain the rules that apply.

- **Rewrite Sentences**: Rewrite sentences to correct errors and improve clarity. Focus on different aspects, such as verb tense consistency or proper comma usage.

Paragraph Editing

- **Edit Paragraphs**: Edit paragraphs for grammatical accuracy and punctuation. This practice helps you apply rules in a more comprehensive context.

- **Use Prompts**: Write paragraphs based on prompts and then revise them, focusing on grammar and punctuation. Review the revisions to understand the improvements made.

Grammar and Punctuation Rules	Examples
Sentence Structure	
Use complete sentences with a subject and a predicate.	She ran. (correct) Ran. (incorrect)
Use proper subject-verb agreement.	He is happy. (correct) He are happy. (incorrect)
Use parallel structure in lists and comparisons.	I like running, swimming, and biking. (correct) I like running, swimming, and to bike. (incorrect)
Punctuation	
Use periods at the end of declarative sentences and abbreviations.	She went to the store. Mr. Smith is here.

Use question marks at the end of direct questions.	What time is it?
Use exclamation points to show strong emotion.	That's amazing!
Use commas to separate items in a list, before conjunctions in compound sentences, and after introductory phrases.	I bought apples, bananas, and oranges. I wanted to go, but it was raining. After the game, we went home.
Use semicolons to join closely related independent clauses and items in a complex list.	I have a big test tomorrow; I can't go out tonight. The winners were John, the team captain; Sarah, the top scorer; and Michael, the most valuable player.
Use colons to introduce lists and explanations.	You'll need the following items: pen, paper, and a calculator.
Use quotation marks around direct speech and titles of short works.	"I'll be there soon," she said. Have you read "The Cask of Amontillado"?
Use apostrophes to show possession and in contractions.	The student's book. She couldn't find her keys.
Commonly Confused Words	
Use "there" to refer to a place, "their" to show possession, and "they're" as a contraction of "they are."	Let's go there. Their car is red. They're going to the party.
Use "your" to show possession and "you're" as a contraction of "you are."	Is this your pen? You're going to love this movie!
Use "its" to show possession and "it's" as a contraction of "it is" or "it has."	The dog wagged its tail. It's been a long day.
Use "affect" as a verb and "effect" as a noun.	The weather will affect our plans. The medicine had no effect.

By mastering grammar and punctuation, you will significantly enhance the clarity and professionalism of your writing. These skills are not only essential for the GED test but also valuable in academic and professional settings. Next, we'll explore Sample Questions and Answer Explanations, where you'll practice applying these skills in a test-like environment and learn from detailed explanations.

Common Pitfalls and Errors to Avoid in the RLA Test

As you prepare for the Reasoning Through Language Arts (RLA) section of the GED test, it's essential to be aware of common pitfalls and errors that can hinder your performance. By understanding these potential challenges, you can take proactive steps to avoid them and demonstrate your mastery of reading, writing, and grammatical skills. Let's explore some of the most common pitfalls and errors to watch out for in each component of the RLA test.

In the reading comprehension component, one common pitfall is failing to read the passages carefully and thoroughly. Skimming or rushing through the text can lead to missing crucial details and misinterpreting the main ideas. To avoid this, take your time and practice active reading strategies, such as underlining key points and making brief notes in the margins. Another error to avoid is answering questions based on personal opinions or assumptions rather than the information provided in the passage. Always refer back to the text and use evidence from the passage to support your answers.

When it comes to the writing and text structure component, a common mistake is neglecting to plan and organize your essay before starting to write. Jumping straight into writing without a clear outline can result in a disjointed and poorly structured response. To prevent this, take a few minutes to brainstorm your ideas, create a rough outline, and ensure that your essay has a logical flow. Another pitfall is failing to address all parts of the writing prompt or going off-topic. Carefully read the prompt and make sure your response directly addresses the question or task at hand.

In the grammar and punctuation component, a frequent error is overlooking subject-verb agreement. Ensure that singular subjects are paired with singular verbs and plural subjects with plural verbs. Pay close attention to compound subjects and collective nouns, which can be tricky. Another common mistake is misusing homophones, such as "their," "there," and "they're," or "your" and "you're." Double-check your word choice and make sure you are using the correct form for the context. Additionally, be mindful of punctuation rules, particularly the use of commas, semicolons, and apostrophes. Review the rules for each punctuation mark and practice applying them correctly in your writing.

Lastly, in the extended response section, a significant pitfall is failing to provide sufficient evidence and examples to support your arguments. While it's important to express your viewpoint, you must back it up with relevant facts, details, or personal experiences. Aim to include at least two or three specific examples to strengthen your position. Another error to avoid is neglecting to proofread and edit your essay. Leave a few minutes at the end to review your work, checking for clarity, coherence, and any grammatical or spelling errors. Reading your essay aloud can help you catch awkward phrasing or sentences that don't flow smoothly.

By being mindful of these common pitfalls and errors, you can approach the RLA test with greater confidence and precision. Take the time to practice identifying and correcting these mistakes in your own reading and writing. Seek feedback from others, such as teachers, tutors, or study partners, who can point out areas for improvement. Remember, the more you practice and refine your skills, the better equipped you'll be to avoid these pitfalls and demonstrate your proficiency in the RLA section of the GED test.

Sample Questions and Answer Explanations

Practicing with sample questions and understanding their explanations is an effective way to prepare for the Reasoning Through Language Arts (RLA) section of the GED test. This approach not only familiarizes you with the test format but also helps reinforce the concepts and skills you need to succeed. In this section, we will provide a variety of sample questions, followed by detailed explanations of the answers. This will help you understand why certain answers are correct and learn from any mistakes.

Sample Reading Comprehension Questions

Passage: *The sun had just set, casting a golden hue across the horizon. Jane sat on the porch, sipping her tea, and reflecting on the day's events. The tranquil scene was a stark contrast to the bustling city life she had left behind.*

Question 1: What is the main idea of the passage?

A. Jane is contemplating moving back to the city.

B. Jane is enjoying a peaceful evening after a busy day.

C. The city is bustling and lively.

D. The sun is setting over the city.

Answer Explanation: The main idea of the passage is B. Jane is enjoying a peaceful evening after a busy day. The passage describes Jane sitting on the porch, sipping tea, and reflecting on the day's events, highlighting the tranquility of her evening.

Question 2: What does the phrase "casting a golden hue across the horizon" suggest about the time of day?

A. It is early morning.

B. It is midday.

C. It is sunset.

D. It is nighttime.

Answer Explanation: The phrase "casting a golden hue across the horizon" suggests C. It is sunset. The description indicates that the sun is setting, creating a golden color in the sky.

Sample Writing and Text Structure Questions

Passage: *Technology has significantly changed the way we communicate. In the past, letters were the primary means of long-distance communication. Today, however, we can instantly connect with anyone around the world through email, social media, and video calls.*

Question 1: What organizational pattern is used in the passage?

A. Cause and effect
B. Compare and contrast
C. Chronological order
D. Problem and solution

Answer Explanation: The organizational pattern used in the passage is B. Compare and contrast. The passage compares the past method of communication (letters) with the current methods (email, social media, and video calls).

Question 2: Which sentence best supports the idea that technology has improved communication?

A. Letters were the primary means of long-distance communication.

B. Technology has significantly changed the way we communicate.

C. We can instantly connect with anyone around the world through email, social media, and video calls.

D. In the past, letters were used to communicate over long distances.

Answer Explanation: The sentence that best supports the idea that technology has improved communication is C. We can instantly connect with anyone around the world through email, social media, and video calls. This sentence provides specific examples of how technology enables instant communication.

Sample Grammar and Punctuation Questions

Question 1: Choose the sentence with the correct punctuation.

A. Jane said "I am going to the store."

B. Jane said, "I am going to the store".

C. Jane said, "I am going to the store."

D. Jane said "I am going to the store".

Answer Explanation: The sentence with the correct punctuation is C. Jane said, "I am going to the store." The comma is placed after "said," and the period is inside the quotation marks.

Question 2: Identify the error in the following sentence: *Each of the students have their own locker.*
A. Each

B. of the students

C. have

D. their own locker

Answer Explanation: The error in the sentence is C. have. The correct verb should be "has" because "each" is a singular subject. The corrected sentence is: Each of the students has their own locker.

Sample Extended Response Question

Prompt: *In recent years, the popularity of electric vehicles (EVs) has increased significantly. Write an essay discussing the benefits and challenges of adopting electric vehicles. Use evidence and examples to support your points.*

Answer Explanation: To respond effectively to this prompt, you should structure your essay as follows:

Introduction:

- Introduce the topic of electric vehicles.
- State your thesis, outlining the main benefits and challenges of EV adoption.

Body Paragraphs:

1. **Benefits of Electric Vehicles**:

   o   Discuss environmental benefits (e.g., reduced emissions, less pollution).

   o   Highlight economic benefits (e.g., lower fuel costs, government incentives).

   o   Provide examples and evidence to support your points.

2. **Challenges of Electric Vehicles**:

   o   Address infrastructure challenges (e.g., charging stations, battery disposal).

   o   Discuss economic challenges (e.g., higher initial cost, limited range).

   o   Provide examples and evidence to support your points.

Conclusion:

- Summarize the main points discussed in the essay.

- Restate the thesis in a new way, reinforcing the importance of understanding both benefits and challenges.

Sample Response: The essay should begin with an engaging introduction that captures the reader's interest. The body paragraphs should provide detailed analysis and evidence for both the benefits and challenges of electric vehicles. The conclusion should effectively summarize the discussion and restate the importance of the topic.

By practicing with sample questions and understanding the detailed explanations of the answers, you can develop a deeper understanding of the types of questions you'll encounter on the GED test and the reasoning behind the correct answers. This approach not only helps you prepare more effectively but also builds your confidence in tackling various question types. Next, we'll explore the Extended Response section in more detail, providing techniques and examples to help you excel in writing coherent and persuasive essays.

CHAPTER 3
REASONING THROUGH LANGUAGE ARTS (RLA)

Extended Response: Techniques and Examples

The Extended Response section of the Reasoning Through Language Arts (RLA) test is one of the most challenging components, requiring you to write a coherent, well-structured essay in response to a prompt. This section evaluates your ability to construct a logical argument, use evidence effectively, and write clearly and persuasively. Here, we'll explore techniques for writing strong extended responses and provide examples to illustrate these strategies.

Understanding the Prompt

Before you begin writing, it's crucial to fully understand the prompt. Here's how to approach it:

1. **Read the Prompt Carefully**: Identify the main question or task. Look for keywords that indicate what you need to do, such as "discuss," "analyze," "compare," or "argue."

2. **Highlight Key Points**: Underline or highlight important words or phrases in the prompt. This helps you stay focused on the task at hand.

3. **Determine the Purpose**: Understand what the prompt is asking you to accomplish. Are you being asked to take a position, explain a concept, or compare two viewpoints?

Planning Your Response

Effective planning is essential for writing a coherent and well-organized essay. Follow these steps:

1. **Brainstorm Ideas**: Spend a few minutes brainstorming ideas related to the prompt. Write down any arguments, evidence, or examples that come to mind.

2. **Organize Your Thoughts**: Group your ideas into main points that you will develop in your essay. Decide on the order in which you will present these points.

3. **Create an Outline**: Develop a basic outline that includes an introduction, body paragraphs, and a conclusion. This helps ensure that your essay has a clear structure and logical flow.

Writing the Introduction

The introduction sets the tone for your essay and introduces your main argument. Here's how to write a strong introduction:

1. **Hook the Reader**: Start with a hook that grabs the reader's attention. This could be a quote, a question, a startling fact, or a brief anecdote.

2. **Provide Background Information**: Give some context for your essay. Briefly explain the issue or topic you will be addressing.

3. **State Your Thesis**: Clearly state your thesis or main argument. This should be a concise statement that outlines your position or the main points you will discuss in your essay.

Developing Body Paragraphs

Each body paragraph should focus on a single main point that supports your thesis. Follow these steps to develop strong body paragraphs:

1. **Start with a Topic Sentence**: Begin each paragraph with a topic sentence that introduces the main point of the paragraph.

2. **Provide Evidence**: Support your main point with evidence, such as facts, statistics, examples, or quotes. Make sure the evidence is relevant and strengthens your argument.

3. **Analyze the Evidence**: Explain how the evidence supports your main point. Discuss its significance and how it relates to your thesis.

4. **Use Transitions**: Use transition words and phrases to connect ideas within and between paragraphs. This helps maintain a smooth flow and logical progression.

Example of a Body Paragraph:

Topic Sentence: One of the primary benefits of electric vehicles (EVs) is their positive impact on the environment.

Evidence: According to a report by the Environmental Protection Agency (EPA), EVs produce significantly fewer greenhouse gas emissions than traditional gasoline-powered vehicles.

Analysis: This reduction in emissions is crucial in the fight against climate change, as transportation is one of the largest sources of greenhouse gases. By adopting EVs, we can reduce our carbon footprint and contribute to a healthier planet.

Transition: Furthermore, EVs offer economic benefits that make them an attractive option for consumers.

Writing the Conclusion

The conclusion wraps up your essay and reinforces your main points. Here's how to write an effective conclusion:

1. **Summarize Main Points**: Briefly summarize the main points you discussed in your body paragraphs.

2. **Restate Your Thesis**: Restate your thesis in a new way, reinforcing the argument you made in your essay.

3. **Leave a Lasting Impression**: End with a final thought or call to action that leaves a lasting impression on the reader. This could be a recommendation, a prediction, or a reflection on the broader implications of your argument.

Example of a Conclusion:

In conclusion, the adoption of electric vehicles presents significant environmental and economic benefits. By reducing greenhouse gas emissions and offering cost savings on fuel and maintenance, EVs are a sustainable and practical solution for the future of transportation. It is imperative that we continue to support and invest in this technology to ensure a cleaner, healthier planet for future generations.

Practice with Sample Prompts

To improve your extended response skills, practice writing essays in response to sample prompts. Here's a step-by-step approach:

1. **Read the Prompt**: Carefully read the prompt and identify the task.

2. **Plan Your Response**: Spend a few minutes brainstorming ideas and creating an outline.

3. **Write the Essay**: Write your essay following the structure outlined above.

4. **Review and Revise**: After writing, review your essay for clarity, coherence, and correctness. Make any necessary revisions to improve your response.

Sample Prompt:

Many people believe that access to technology has improved education, while others argue that it has created new challenges. Write an essay discussing both perspectives and provide your own viewpoint on the impact of technology on education.

Sample Response:

Introduction: Technology has revolutionized many aspects of our lives, including education. While some argue that access to technology has enhanced learning opportunities, others contend that it has introduced new challenges. This essay will discuss both perspectives and provide an evaluation of the overall impact of technology on education.

Body Paragraph 1: On one hand, technology has significantly improved education by providing access to a vast array of resources. Online courses, educational apps, and digital textbooks offer students and teachers a wealth of information at their fingertips. For example, platforms like Khan Academy provide free educational content that can be accessed from anywhere in the world, making education more inclusive and accessible.

Body Paragraph 2: On the other hand, the integration of technology in education has introduced challenges such as digital distractions and unequal access. Students may be tempted to use their devices for non-educational purposes, leading to decreased focus and productivity. Additionally, the digital divide means that not all students have equal access to technology, which can exacerbate existing educational inequalities.

Conclusion: In conclusion, while technology has undeniably transformed education by increasing access to resources and opportunities, it also presents challenges that must be addressed. By finding a balance between leveraging technological advancements and mitigating their drawbacks, we can harness the full potential of technology to enhance education for all.

By practicing these techniques and writing responses to sample prompts, you will develop the skills needed to craft well-organized, coherent, and persuasive essays for the GED test. The ability to write effectively is not only crucial for the test but also a valuable skill for academic and professional success.

CHAPTER 4
MATHEMATICAL REASONING

The Mathematical Reasoning section of the GED test is designed to assess your understanding and application of fundamental mathematical concepts. This section covers a wide range of topics, including algebra, geometry, and arithmetic. Mastering these concepts is crucial not only for passing the GED test but also for everyday problem-solving and critical thinking. In this chapter, we will explore each major area of the Mathematical Reasoning section, providing comprehensive explanations, practical examples, and strategies to help you succeed.

Section Overview

The Mathematical Reasoning section is structured to evaluate your ability to solve mathematical problems using both algebraic and quantitative reasoning skills. This section is divided into two parts: one that allows the use of a calculator and one that does not. The questions are designed to test your understanding of mathematical principles and your ability to apply them to real-world scenarios.

Test Structure and Timing

- **Duration**: The entire Mathematical Reasoning section lasts 115 minutes.

- **Calculator Use**: You can use the TI-30XS MultiView calculator for part of the section, while the other part must be completed without a calculator.

- **Question Types**: The section includes multiple-choice questions, drag-and-drop, drop-down, fill-in-the-blank, and hot spot questions. These varied formats assess your ability to perform calculations, interpret data, and solve problems.

- **Scoring**: Each question in the Mathematical Reasoning section contributes to your overall score, which ranges from 100 to 200. A passing score of 145 is required.

Skills Assessed

The Mathematical Reasoning section covers several key areas, each designed to test different skills:

- **Algebra**: Equations and expressions, solving linear equations, systems of equations, and inequalities.

- **Geometry**: Understanding properties of geometric figures, calculating measurements, and applying geometric principles to solve problems.

- **Arithmetic**: Basic arithmetic operations, percentages, proportions, ratios, and interpreting quantitative data.

- **Data Analysis**: Interpreting graphs, charts, and tables, and using data to make informed decisions.

Preparation Tips

To excel in the Mathematical Reasoning section, it's important to develop a systematic approach to studying and practicing:

1. **Review Fundamental Concepts**: Ensure you have a solid understanding of basic mathematical principles before tackling more complex problems.

2. **Practice Regularly**: Consistent practice is key to retaining mathematical concepts and improving problem-solving skills. Use practice tests and exercises to identify areas where you need improvement.

3. **Utilize Resources**: Take advantage of study guides, online tutorials, and educational apps to reinforce your learning. The TI-30XS MultiView calculator is a valuable tool—practice using it to become familiar with its functions.

4. **Manage Your Time**: Develop time management strategies to ensure you can complete all questions within the allotted time. Practice under timed conditions to build your test-taking stamina.

By understanding the structure and requirements of the Mathematical Reasoning section, you can approach your preparation with confidence and focus. Let's delve deeper into each major area, starting with Algebra: Equations and Expressions.

Algebra: Equations and Expressions

Algebra forms the foundation of the Mathematical Reasoning section and is essential for solving a wide range of mathematical problems. This section will cover key algebraic concepts, including equations, expressions, and their applications.

Equations and Expressions

- **Understanding Variables**: Variables are symbols used to represent unknown values in equations and expressions. Familiarize yourself with common variables such as x, y, and z.

- **Writing Equations**: Learn how to translate word problems into algebraic equations. This skill involves identifying key information and representing it mathematically.

- **Solving Linear Equations**: Practice solving linear equations, which are equations of the first degree (e.g., $2x + 3 = 7$). Master techniques such as isolating variables and using inverse operations.

- **Systems of Equations**: Understand how to solve systems of equations, where two or more equations are solved simultaneously. Techniques include substitution, elimination, and graphing.

- **Inequalities**: Study how to solve and graph inequalities, which involve expressions that use inequality symbols (e.g., $>, <, \geq, \leq$). Learn how to manipulate inequalities and represent solutions on a number line.

Practice Problems

To reinforce your understanding of algebraic concepts, solve practice problems regularly.

Here are some examples:

1. **Solve for x**: $2x + 5 = 15$
   - Solution: Subtract 5 from both sides: $2x = 10$
   - Divide by 2: $x = 5$

2. **Solve the system of equations**: $x + y = 10$ $x - y = 4$
   - Solution: Add the equations to eliminate y: $2x = 14$
   - Divide by 2: $x = 7$
   - Substitute x back into $x + y = 10$: $7 + y = 10$
   - Solve for y: $y = 3$
   - Solution: $x = 7, y = 3$

3. **Graph the inequality**: $2x - 3 > 1$
   - Solution: Add 3 to both sides: $2x > 4$
   - Divide by 2: $x > 2$

o   Graph $x > 2$ on a number line: Shade the region to the right of 2, with an open circle at 2.

By mastering these algebraic techniques and practicing regularly, you will develop the skills needed to tackle algebra problems confidently and accurately. Next, we will explore Geometry: Figures and Measurements, where you'll learn to understand geometric properties and apply them to solve practical problems.

Algebra: Equations and Expressions

Algebra is a fundamental component of the Mathematical Reasoning section of the GED test. It involves understanding and manipulating mathematical symbols to solve equations and expressions. Mastering algebraic concepts is crucial for tackling a wide range of problems in this section. In this segment, we will delve into key algebraic topics, providing detailed explanations and practical examples to help you develop your skills.

Understanding Variables and Constants

Variables are symbols, usually letters, that represent unknown values in mathematical expressions and equations. Constants are fixed values. Together, they form the basis of algebraic expressions and equations.

Examples:

- Variables: x, y, z

- Constants: 2, -5, 3.14

Writing and Simplifying Algebraic Expressions

Algebraic expressions are combinations of variables, constants, and operators (such as +, -, *, /). Simplifying these expressions involves combining like terms and applying mathematical operations.

Example: Simplify the expression: $3x + 5x - 2 + 7$

- Combine like terms: $3x + 5x = 8x$

- Combine constants: $-2 + 7 = 5$

- Simplified expression: $8x + 5$

Solving Linear Equations

Linear equations are equations of the first degree, meaning they involve variables raised to the power of one. Solving these equations involves isolating the variable on one side of the equation.

Example: Solve for x: $2x + 3 = 11$

- Subtract 3 from both sides: $2x = 8$

- Divide by 2: $x = 4$

Steps:

1. Simplify both sides of the equation if necessary.

2. Use inverse operations to isolate the variable.

3. Check your solution by substituting it back into the original equation.

Solving Systems of Equations

A system of equations involves solving two or more equations simultaneously. Common methods include substitution and elimination.

Example: Solve the system of equations: $x + y = 10 \; x - y = 4$

Using Substitution:

1. Solve one equation for one variable: $x = y + 4$ (from the second equation).

2. Substitute this expression into the other equation: $(y + 4) + y = 10$.

3. Simplify and solve for y: $2y + 4 = 10 \rightarrow 2y = 6 \rightarrow y = 3$.

4. Substitute y back into the first equation: $x + 3 = 10 \rightarrow x = 7$.

Solution: $x = 7, y = 3$

Solving and Graphing Inequalities

Inequalities express a relationship where one side is not necessarily equal to the other but could be greater or less. Solving inequalities involves similar steps to solving equations but requires careful attention to the direction of the inequality.

Example: Solve and graph the inequality: $3x - 4 < 5$

- Add 4 to both sides: $3x < 9$

- Divide by 3: $x < 3$

To graph this on a number line:

- Draw a number line.

- Place an open circle at 3 to indicate that 3 is not included.

- Shade the region to the left of 3 to represent all values less than 3.

Practical Applications

Algebra is not just about solving abstract problems; it has practical applications in various fields such as science, engineering, economics, and everyday life. Here are a few examples:

- **Budgeting**: Algebra can help you manage finances by creating and solving equations related to income and expenses.

- **Construction**: Engineers use algebraic equations to calculate materials needed and ensure structural integrity.

- **Science**: Scientists use algebra to analyze data, model relationships, and predict outcomes.

Practice Problems

To reinforce your understanding, solve these practice problems:

1. Simplify the expression: $4y - 2y + 7 - 3$

   o Solution: $2y + 4$

2. Solve for x: $5x - 7 = 18$

   o Solution: $x = 5$

3. Solve the system of equations: $2x + y = 7$ $3x - y = 8$

   o Solution: $x = 3, y = 1$

4. Solve and graph the inequality: $2x + 3 \geq 7$

   o Solution: $x \geq 2$

By practicing these algebraic techniques and understanding their applications, you will build a strong foundation for solving a wide range of mathematical problems. Next, we will explore Geometry: Figures and Measurements, where you will learn to understand geometric properties and apply them to solve practical problems.

Geometry: Figures and Measurements

Geometry is a vital area of mathematics that deals with the properties and relationships of shapes, sizes, and the relative positions of figures. In the Mathematical Reasoning section of the GED test, you will encounter various geometric concepts that require you to analyze and solve problems involving different types of figures and measurements. This section will guide you through the essential concepts of geometry, providing detailed explanations and practical examples to enhance your understanding.

Understanding Basic Geometric Figures

To excel in geometry, you need to be familiar with the basic types of geometric figures and their properties. Here are some fundamental shapes and their characteristics:

Points, Lines, and Planes

- **Point**: A location in space with no dimensions (length, width, or height).
- **Line**: A straight one-dimensional figure that extends infinitely in both directions.
- **Plane**: A flat two-dimensional surface that extends infinitely in all directions.

Angles

- **Acute Angle**: An angle less than 90 degrees.
- **Right Angle**: An angle exactly 90 degrees.
- **Obtuse Angle**: An angle greater than 90 degrees but less than 180 degrees.
- **Straight Angle**: An angle exactly 180 degrees.

Triangles

- **Equilateral Triangle**: All sides and angles are equal.
- **Isosceles Triangle**: Two sides and two angles are equal.
- **Scalene Triangle**: All sides and angles are different.
- **Right Triangle**: Has one 90-degree angle.

Quadrilaterals

- **Square**: All sides and angles are equal, with each angle being 90 degrees.
- **Rectangle**: Opposite sides are equal, and all angles are 90 degrees.
- **Parallelogram**: Opposite sides are parallel and equal.
- **Trapezoid**: Only one pair of opposite sides is parallel.

Calculating Perimeter and Area

Perimeter and area are two fundamental measurements in geometry. Here's how to calculate them for various shapes:

Perimeter

- **Rectangle**: $P = 2 * (length + width)$
- **Square**: $P = 4 * side$
- **Triangle**: $P = side1 + side2 + side3$

Area

- **Rectangle**: $A = length * width$
- **Square**: $A = side * side$
- **Triangle**: $A = \left(\frac{1}{2}\right) * base * height$
- **Circle**: $A = pi * radius2$

Examples:

1. Find the perimeter and area of a rectangle with a length of 8 units and a width of 5 units.
   - Perimeter: $P = 2 * (8 + 5) = 26\, units$
   - Area: $A = 8 * 5 = 40\, square\ units$

2. Find the area of a triangle with a base of 10 units and a height of 6 units.
   - Area: $A = \left(\frac{1}{2}\right) * 10 * 6 = 30\, square\ units$

Understanding Circles

Circles have unique properties and measurements. Key terms include:

- **Radius**: The distance from the center to any point on the circle.
- **Diameter**: Twice the radius, or the distance across the circle through the center.
- **Circumference**: The distance around the circle.
- **Pi (п)**: Approximately 3.14159, a constant representing the ratio of a circle's circumference to its diameter.

Formulas:

- **Circumference**: $C = 2 * pi * radius$
- **Area**: $A = pi * radius2$

Example: Find the circumference and area of a circle with a radius of 7 units.

CHAPTER 4
MATHEMATICAL REASONING

- Circumference: $C = 2 * pi * 7 \approx 44\ units$
- Area: $A = pi * 72 \approx 154\ square\ units$

Understanding Volume and Surface Area

Volume and surface area are critical measurements for three-dimensional figures. Here's how to calculate them:

Volume

- **Rectangular Prism**: $V = length * width * height$
- **Cylinder**: $V = pi * radius2 * height$
- **Sphere**: $V = \left(\frac{4}{3}\right) * pi * radius3$

Surface Area

- **Rectangular Prism**: $SA = 2 * (length * width + length * height + width * height)$
- **Cylinder**: $SA = 2 * pi * radius * (height + radius)$
- **Sphere**: $SA = 4 * pi * radius2$

Examples:

1. Find the volume and surface area of a rectangular prism with a length of 5 units, a width of 3 units, and a height of 4 units.

    o   Volume: $V = 5 * 3 * 4 = 60\ cubic\ units$

    o   Surface Area: SA = 2 * (5 * 3 + 5 * 4 + 3 * 4) = 94 $square\ units$

2. Find the volume of a cylinder with a radius of 3 units and a height of 10 units.

    o   Volume: $V = pi * 32 * 10 \approx 282.74\ cubic\ units$

Practical Applications

Geometry is not just about abstract concepts; it has numerous practical applications in fields such as engineering, architecture, art, and everyday life. Here are some examples:

- **Architecture**: Architects use geometric principles to design buildings and structures, ensuring stability and aesthetic appeal.

- **Engineering**: Engineers apply geometry to design and analyze mechanical systems, electrical circuits, and infrastructure projects.

- **Art**: Artists use geometric shapes and principles to create visually appealing compositions.

- **Daily Life**: Geometry helps in various daily tasks, such as arranging furniture, designing spaces, and understanding spatial relationships.

Practice Problems

To reinforce your understanding of geometric concepts, solve these practice problems:

1. Find the perimeter and area of a square with a side length of 6 units.

   o Perimeter: $P = 4 * 6 = 24 \, units$

   o Area: $A = 6 * 6 = 36 \, square \, units$

2. Calculate the volume of a sphere with a radius of 4 units.

   o Volume: $V = \left(\frac{4}{3}\right) * pi * 43 \approx 268.08 \, cubic \, units$

3. Determine the surface area of a cylinder with a radius of 5 units and a height of 12 units.

   o Surface Area: $SA = 2 * pi * 5 * (12 + 5) \approx 534.07 \, square \, units$

By mastering these geometric concepts and practicing regularly, you will develop the skills needed to solve a wide range of geometric problems confidently and accurately. Next, we will explore Arithmetic: Percentages and Proportions, where you will learn to understand and apply arithmetic principles to solve practical problems.

Arithmetic: Percentages and Proportions

Arithmetic forms the backbone of many mathematical concepts and everyday calculations. Understanding percentages and proportions is essential for solving a variety of real-world problems, from calculating discounts to mixing ingredients in recipes. In this section, we will explore the concepts of percentages and proportions, providing detailed explanations and practical examples to help you master these topics.

Understanding Percentages

A percentage is a way of expressing a number as a fraction of 100. Percentages are used to compare quantities, calculate increases or decreases, and understand proportions in a straightforward manner.

Basic Concepts

- **Percent**: The term "percent" means "per hundred." For example, 50% means 50 out of 100, or 50/100, which simplifies to 0.5.

- **Converting Fractions to Percentages**: Multiply the fraction by 100. For example, 1/4 = 0.25, and 0.25 * 100 = 25%.

- **Converting Decimals to Percentages**: Multiply the decimal by 100. For example, 0.75 * 100 = 75%.

Calculating Percentages

1. **Finding a Percentage of a Number**: Multiply the number by the percentage (as a decimal).

   o Example: What is 20% of 50?

     ▪ 20% = 0.20

     ▪ 0.20 * 50 = 10

2. **Finding the Whole from a Percentage**: Divide the part by the percentage (as a decimal).

   o Example: If 15 is 30% of a number, what is the whole number?

     ▪ 30% = 0.30

     ▪ 15/0.30 = 50

3. **Finding the Percentage Increase or Decrease**:

   o **Increase**: ((new value - original value)/original value) * 100

   o **Decrease**: ((original value - new value)/original value) * 100 o   Example: If a product's price increases from $40 to $50, what is the percentage increase?

- ((50 - 40)/40) * 100 = (10/40) * 100 = 25%

Understanding Proportions

A proportion is an equation that states two ratios are equal. Proportions are used to solve problems involving scaling, mixing, and comparisons.

Basic Concepts

- **Ratio**: A ratio is a comparison of two quantities. For example, the ratio of 2 to 3 can be written as 2:3 or 2/3.

- **Proportion**: A proportion states that two ratios are equal. For example, if 2/3 = 4/6, then these ratios are proportional.

Solving Proportions To solve proportions, use cross-multiplication. If a/b = c/d, then ad = bc.

Examples:

1. Solve the proportion for x: ¾ $= \frac{x}{8}$

   o   Cross-multiply: $3 * 8 = 4 * x$

   o $24 = 4x$

   o   Divide by 4: $x = 6$

2. Determine if the following ratios are proportional: $\frac{5}{6}$ and $\frac{10}{12}$

   o   Cross-multiply: $5 * 12 = 6 * 10$

   o $60 = 60$ (Since the products are equal, the ratios are proportional.)

Practical Applications

Percentages and proportions are widely used in various fields and everyday situations:

Finance and Shopping

- **Interest Rates**: Understanding percentages helps in calculating interest rates on loans and savings.

- **Discounts**: Calculating sale prices using percentages.

- Example: A $120 jacket is on sale for 25% off. What is the sale price?

  - 25% of $120 = 0.25 * 120 = $30

  - Sale price = $120 - $30 = $90

Cooking and Recipes

- **Scaling Recipes**: Using proportions to adjust ingredient quantities.

  - Example: A recipe for 4 servings requires 2 cups of flour. How much flour is needed for 6 servings?

    - Set up a proportion: $\frac{2}{4} = \frac{x}{6}$

    - Cross-multiply: $2 * 6 = 4 * x$

    - $12 = 4x$

    - Divide by 4: $x = 3 \ cups$

Health and Fitness

- **Body Mass Index (BMI)**: Calculating BMI using height and weight proportions.

  - Example: A person weighing 150 pounds and measuring 68 inches tall has a BMI calculated as follows:

    - BMI = (weight in pounds/height in inches^2) * 703

    - BMI = $(150/68^2) * 703 \approx 22.8$

Practice Problems

To reinforce your understanding of percentages and proportions, solve these practice problems:

1. **Find the percentage of a number**: What is 15% of 200?

   - Solution: 15% = 0.15

   - 0.15 * 200 = 30

2. **Solve the proportion for x**: $\frac{4}{5} = \frac{x}{10}$

   - Solution: Cross-multiply: 4 * 10 = 5 * x

   - 40 = 5x

   - Divide by 5: x = 8

3. **Calculate the percentage decrease**: A TV originally priced at $500 is now $400. What is the percentage decrease?

   o   Solution: $((500 - 400)/500) * 100 = (100/500) * 100 = 20\%$

By mastering these arithmetic principles and practicing regularly, you will develop the skills needed to solve a wide range of practical problems confidently and accurately. Next, we will explore Sample Questions and Answer Explanations, where you will practice applying these skills in a test-like environment and learn from detailed explanations.

Sample Questions and Answer Explanations

Practicing with sample questions and understanding their explanations is a crucial part of preparing for the Mathematical Reasoning section of the GED test. This approach helps you familiarize yourself with the types of questions you will encounter, improve your problem-solving skills, and build confidence. In this section, we provide a variety of sample questions, followed by detailed explanations of the answers, to help you master the concepts covered in this chapter.

Sample Question 1: Algebra

Question: Solve for x in the equation $3x - 5 = 16$.

Solution:

1. Add 5 to both sides of the equation to isolate the term with the variable: $3x - 5 + 5 = 16 + 5$ $3x = 21$

2. Divide both sides by 3 to solve for x: $\frac{3x}{3} = \frac{21}{3}$ $x = 7$

Answer: x = 7

Explanation: The steps to isolate the variable involve first eliminating the constant on the left side by adding 5 to both sides, then solving for the variable by dividing both sides by the coefficient of x, which is 3.

Sample Question 2: Geometry

Question: Calculate the area of a triangle with a base of 8 units and a height of 5 units.

Solution:

1. Use the formula for the area of a triangle: $Area = \left(\frac{1}{2}\right) * base * height$

2. Substitute the given values: $Area = \left(\frac{1}{2}\right) * 8 * 5$ $Area = 4 * 5$ $Area = 20\ square\ units$

Answer: 20 square units

Explanation: The area of a triangle is found by multiplying the base by the height and then dividing by 2. This formula applies to all triangles, making it a fundamental concept in geometry.

Sample Question 3: Arithmetic - Percentages

Question: What is 15% of 250?

Solution:

1. Convert the percentage to a decimal: 15% = 0.15

CHAPTER 4
MATHEMATICAL REASONING

2. Multiply the decimal by the number: 0.15 * 250 = 37.5

Answer: 37.5

Explanation: Converting the percentage to a decimal simplifies the calculation. Multiplying the decimal by the total number gives the part represented by the percentage.

Sample Question 4: Proportions

Question: Solve the proportion for x: $\frac{7}{9} = \frac{x}{27}$.

Solution:

1. Use cross-multiplication to solve the proportion: $7 * 27 = 9 * x$ $189 = 9x$

2. Divide both sides by 9 to solve for x: $\frac{189}{9} = x$ $x = 21$

Answer: x = 21

Explanation: Cross-multiplication involves multiplying the numerator of one fraction by the denominator of the other fraction, then setting the two products equal to each other. This method simplifies solving for the unknown variable.

Sample Question 5: Geometry - Volume

Question: Find the volume of a cylinder with a radius of 3 units and a height of 10 units.

Solution:

1. Use the formula for the volume of a cylinder: Volume = pi * radius^2 * height

2. Substitute the given values: Volume = pi * (3^2) * 10 Volume = pi * 9 * 10 Volume = 90pi ≈ 282.74 cubic units

Answer: 282.74 cubic units

Explanation: The volume of a cylinder is calculated by multiplying the area of the base (which is a circle) by the height of the cylinder. Using pi in the calculation ensures accuracy for the circular base.

Sample Question 6: Arithmetic - Percentage Increase

Question: A product's price increased from $80 to $100. What is the percentage increase?

Solution:

1. Calculate the difference in price: Difference = $100 - $80 = $20

2. Divide the difference by the original price and multiply by 100: Percentage Increase = (20/80) * 100 Percentage Increase = 0.25 * 100 Percentage Increase = 25%

Answer: 25%

Explanation: The percentage increase is found by dividing the amount of increase by the original price, then converting the decimal to a percentage by multiplying by 100. This method is widely used in finance and retail to understand price changes.

Sample Question 7: Proportions in Real Life

Question: A recipe calls for 4 cups of flour to make 24 cookies. How much flour is needed to make 60 cookies?

Solution:

1. Set up a proportion to solve for the unknown quantity: $4/24 = x/60$

2. Use cross-multiplication to find x: $4 * 60 = 24 * x$ $240 = 24x$

3. Divide both sides by 24: $x = 240/24$ $x = 10$ cups

Answer: 10 cups

Explanation: Setting up a proportion allows you to scale the recipe up or down while maintaining the same ratio of ingredients. Cross-multiplication and solving for x gives the amount of flour needed for the increased number of cookies.

By practicing these sample questions and thoroughly understanding the explanations, you will strengthen your mathematical reasoning skills and be better prepared for the GED test. Regular practice with a variety of problems helps solidify your understanding and improves your ability to apply mathematical concepts effectively. Next, we will explore using the TI-30XS MultiView Calculator, an essential tool for the GED Mathematical Reasoning section.

Using the TI-30XS MultiView Calculator

The TI-30XS MultiView calculator is an essential tool for the Mathematical Reasoning section of the GED test. This calculator allows you to perform a wide range of mathematical operations efficiently and accurately. Mastering its functions will enable you to solve complex problems with confidence. In this section, we will explore the key features of the TI-30XS MultiView calculator, provide tips for its effective use, and offer examples to illustrate its applications.

Key Features of the TI-30XS MultiView Calculator

The TI-30XS MultiView calculator is designed to handle various mathematical tasks, from basic arithmetic to advanced functions. Here are some of its key features:

MultiView Display

- **Four-Line Display**: Allows you to see multiple calculations and results simultaneously, making it easier to track your work and verify accuracy.

- **Scrolling**: Enables you to scroll through previous entries, which is useful for reviewing and correcting calculations.

Fraction and Decimal Conversion

- **Fraction Simplification**: Simplifies fractions and converts between improper fractions and mixed numbers.

- **Decimal Conversion**: Converts fractions to decimals and vice versa with a single key press.

Scientific Notation

- **Notation Mode**: Easily enter and display numbers in scientific notation, which is essential for handling very large or very small numbers.

Statistical Functions

- **One-Variable Statistics**: Calculate mean, median, mode, and standard deviation.

- **Two-Variable Statistics**: Perform linear regression and correlation calculations.

Memory and Constants

- **Memory Keys**: Store and recall previous calculations, constants, and frequently used numbers.

- **Constant Feature**: Automatically use a stored constant in calculations, such as pi (π) or other constants.

Effective Use of the TI-30XS MultiView Calculator

To maximize the benefits of the TI-30XS MultiView calculator, it's important to become familiar with its functions and practice using it regularly. Here are some tips for effective use:

Familiarize Yourself with the Key Functions

- **Basic Operations**: Ensure you know how to perform basic arithmetic operations (addition, subtraction, multiplication, division).

- **Special Functions**: Learn how to use the fraction, decimal, and percentage keys, as well as functions for square roots, exponents, and logarithms.

Practice with Real Problems

- **Sample Questions**: Use practice questions from this guide and other resources to apply the calculator's functions to real problems.

- **GED Practice Tests**: Take practice tests under timed conditions to simulate the test environment and build confidence in using the calculator efficiently.

Use Memory Features

- **Store Frequently Used Numbers**: Store constants and frequently used numbers in the calculator's memory for quick access.

- **Recall Previous Calculations**: Use the memory recall function to review previous calculations and verify accuracy.

Examples of Using the TI-30XS MultiView Calculator

Here are some examples that illustrate how to use the TI-30XS MultiView calculator for various types of calculations:

Example 1: Basic Arithmetic Calculate $45 + 32/(6 * 2)$

1. Enter: $45 + 32 \div (6 \times 2)$
2. Display: $45 + 32 \div 12$
3. Result: 47.67

Example 2: Fraction to Decimal Conversion Convert 3/8 to a decimal.

1. Enter: $3 \div 8$
2. Display: 0.375

Example 3: Simplifying a Fraction Simplify 36/48.

1. Enter: 36 n/d 48 (n/d is the fraction key)

2. Display: 3/4

Example 4: Calculating Mean and Standard Deviation Given data set: 5, 10, 15, 20

1. Enter: STAT, 1-VAR, input data

2. Display mean ($\bar{x}$): 12.5

3. Display standard deviation (σx): 5.59

Example 5: Using Scientific Notation Calculate $(3.5 \times 10^5) \times (2.1 \times 10^3)$.

1. Enter: $3.5 \times 10^5 \times 2.1 \times 10^3$

2. Display: 7.35×10^8

Example 6: Solving an Algebraic Equation Solve for x: 2x + 3 = 11.

1. Isolate x: 2x = 8

2. Solve: x = 8 ÷ 2

3. Display: 4

Practice Problems

To further enhance your skills, solve the following practice problems using the TI-30XS MultiView calculator:

1. **Percentage Calculation**: Find 25% of 160.

    o Enter: 0.25 × 160

    o Result: 40

2. **Square Root**: Calculate the square root of 144.

    o Enter: $\sqrt{144}$

    o Result: 12

3. **Exponentiation**: Evaluate 5^3.

    o Enter: 5^3

    o Result: 125

4. **Solving Proportions**: Solve for x in the proportion $3/4 = x/8$.

   o   Enter: $3 \times 8 \div 4$

   o   Result: $x = 6$

5. **Statistical Calculation**: Find the mean of the data set 7, 14, 21, 28.

   o   Enter: STAT, 1-VAR, input data

   o   Display mean ($\bar{x}$): 17.5

By mastering the functions and capabilities of the TI-30XS MultiView calculator, you will be able to approach the Mathematical Reasoning section with greater confidence and efficiency. Practice regularly and refer to the user manual as needed to ensure you are utilizing all available features effectively.

CHAPTER 5
SCIENCE

The Science section of the GED test evaluates your understanding of fundamental scientific concepts and your ability to apply scientific reasoning to solve problems. This section covers three main areas: Physical Science, Life Science, and Earth and Space Science. You will encounter a variety of question types, including multiple-choice, drag-and-drop, fill-in-the-blank, and hot spot questions. This chapter provides an in-depth exploration of each scientific domain, offering detailed explanations, practical examples, and strategies to help you excel.

Section Overview

The Science section is designed to assess your ability to understand and analyze scientific information, interpret data, and apply scientific principles to real-world scenarios. Here's an overview of what to expect in this section:

Test Structure and Timing

- **Duration**: The Science section is 90 minutes long.

- **Question Types**: The section includes multiple-choice, drag-and-drop, drop-down, fill-in-the-blank, and hot spot questions. These questions test your ability to analyze and interpret scientific information.

- **Scoring**: Each question in the Science section contributes to your overall score, which ranges from 100 to 200. A passing score of 145 is required.

Skills Assessed

The Science section evaluates several key skills, including:

- **Understanding Scientific Concepts**: Grasping fundamental principles in physics, chemistry, biology, and earth and space science.

- **Interpreting Data**: Analyzing graphs, tables, and diagrams to draw conclusions and make predictions.

- **Applying Scientific Reasoning**: Using scientific principles to solve problems and explain phenomena.

- **Reading Comprehension**: Understanding and interpreting scientific texts and articles.

Preparation Tips

To prepare effectively for the Science section, it's important to develop a systematic approach to studying and practicing:

1. **Review Fundamental Concepts**: Ensure you have a solid understanding of basic scientific principles across all three domains: Physical Science, Life Science, and Earth and Space Science.

2. **Practice Data Interpretation**: Regularly practice interpreting data from graphs, tables, and diagrams. This skill is crucial for answering many questions in the Science section.

3. **Utilize Resources**: Take advantage of study guides, online tutorials, and educational videos to reinforce your learning. The explanations and examples in this book will also help clarify complex topics.

4. **Take Practice Tests**: Complete full-length practice tests under timed conditions to build confidence and improve your test-taking skills. Reviewing your answers and understanding any mistakes is essential for improvement.

By understanding the structure and requirements of the Science section, you can approach your preparation with confidence and focus. Let's delve deeper into each scientific domain, starting with Physical Science: Physics and Chemistry.

Physical Science: Physics and Chemistry

Physical Science encompasses the study of non-living systems and includes the fields of physics and chemistry. This section will cover key concepts, including the properties of matter, chemical reactions, force and motion, and energy transformations. Understanding these principles is essential for analyzing physical phenomena and solving related problems.

Key Topics in Physics

- **Force and Motion**: Study the laws of motion, including Newton's laws, and understand how forces affect the movement of objects.

- **Energy**: Explore different forms of energy (kinetic, potential, thermal, chemical, etc.) and the principles of energy conservation and transfer.

- **Waves**: Learn about the properties of waves, including frequency, wavelength, and amplitude, as well as their applications in sound and light.

- **Electricity and Magnetism**: Understand the principles of electric circuits, electromagnetism, and the behavior of electrical charges.

Key Topics in Chemistry

- **Properties of Matter**: Understand the states of matter (solid, liquid, gas) and their properties, including density, melting point, and boiling point.

- **Chemical Reactions**: Study the types of chemical reactions, balancing chemical equations, and the principles of conservation of mass.

- **Atomic Structure**: Learn about the structure of atoms, including protons, neutrons, and electrons, and how they determine the chemical properties of elements.

- **Periodic Table**: Familiarize yourself with the periodic table, including the organization of elements and periodic trends such as electronegativity and atomic radius.

Practical Applications

Physical science principles are applied in various fields and everyday situations. Here are some examples:

- **Engineering**: Engineers use physics to design structures, vehicles, and machinery, ensuring they operate safely and efficiently.

- **Medicine**: Chemistry is essential in the development of pharmaceuticals and understanding biochemical processes in the human body.

- **Environmental Science**: Understanding chemical reactions and energy transfer is crucial for addressing environmental issues such as pollution and climate change.

Practice Problems

To reinforce your understanding of physical science concepts, solve these practice problems:

1. **Physics - Force and Motion**: Calculate the acceleration of a 10 kg object subjected to a net force of 50 N.

     o   Solution: Use Newton's second law: $F = m * a$

     o $a = F/m = 50 \text{ N}/10 \text{ kg} = 5 \text{ m/s}^2$

2. **Chemistry - Balancing Equations**: Balance the chemical equation for the combustion of methane (CH_4): $CH_4 + O_2 \rightarrow CO_2 + H_2O$.

   o   Solution: Balanced equation: $CH_4 + 2O_2 \rightarrow CO_2 + 2H_2O$

3. **Physics - Energy**: Calculate the kinetic energy of a 2 kg object moving at a velocity of 3 m/s.

   o   Solution: Use the kinetic energy formula: $KE = (1/2) * m * v^2$

   o $KE = 0.5 * 2 \text{ kg} * (3 \text{ m/s})^2 = 0.5 * 2 * 9 = 9 \text{ Joules}$

By mastering these physical science concepts and practicing regularly, you will develop the skills needed to solve a wide range of scientific problems confidently and accurately. Next, we will explore Life Science: Biology, where you will learn to understand biological principles and their applications.

Physical Science: Physics and Chemistry

Physical Science encompasses the study of non-living systems, focusing on the fundamental principles of physics and chemistry. This section will cover key concepts in both fields, providing a comprehensive understanding that is essential for analyzing physical phenomena and solving related problems. We will explore the properties of matter, chemical reactions, force and motion, energy transformations, and more.

Key Concepts in Physics

Physics is the study of matter, energy, and the interactions between them. Here are some of the fundamental topics you need to master:

Force and Motion

- **Newton's Laws of Motion**: These laws describe the relationship between a body and the forces acting upon it, and its motion in response to those forces.

    o **First Law (Inertia)**: An object at rest stays at rest, and an object in motion stays in motion unless acted upon by an external force.

    o **Second Law (F = ma)**: The acceleration of an object is directly proportional to the net force acting on it and inversely proportional to its mass.

    o **Third Law (Action and Reaction)**: For every action, there is an equal and opposite reaction.

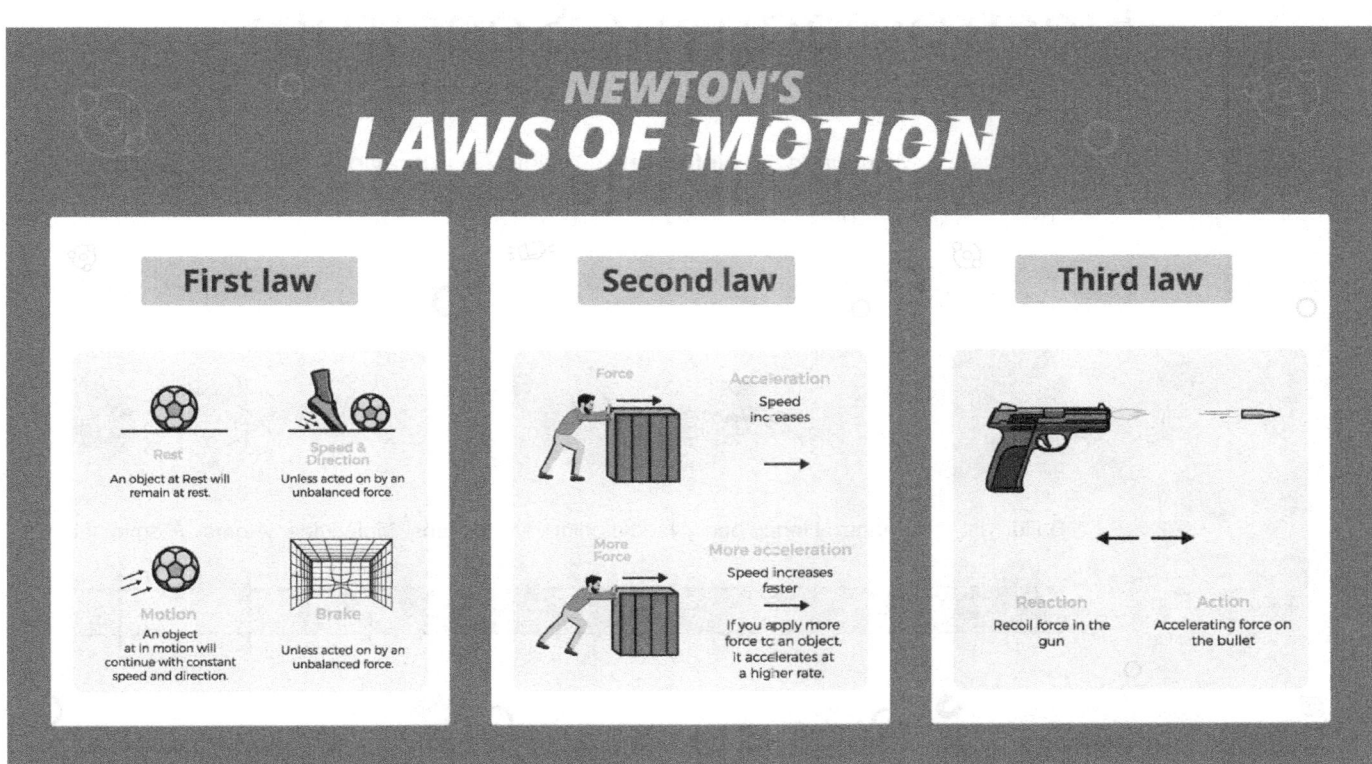

- **Kinematics**: The study of motion without considering its causes, including concepts such as velocity, acceleration, and displacement.

- **Dynamics**: The study of the forces and their impact on motion.

Energy

- **Types of Energy**: Energy exists in various forms, including kinetic, potential, thermal, chemical, and more.

    - **Kinetic Energy (KE)**: The energy of motion, calculated using the formula $KE = (1/2) * m * v^2$.

    - **Potential Energy (PE)**: The stored energy of position, calculated using $PE = m * g * h$, where m is mass, g is acceleration due to gravity, and h is height.

- **Conservation of Energy**: The principle that energy cannot be created or destroyed, only transformed from one form to another.

Waves

- **Properties of Waves**: Includes frequency, wavelength, amplitude, and speed.

- **Types of Waves**: Mechanical waves (such as sound waves) and electromagnetic waves (such as light waves).

- **Wave Behavior**: Reflection, refraction, diffraction, and interference.

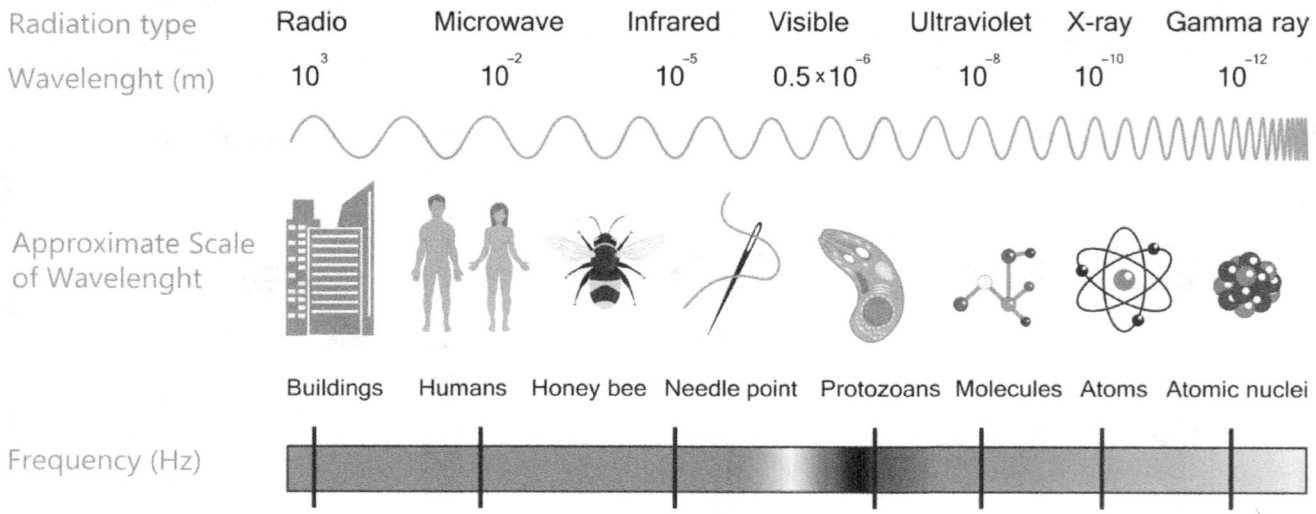

Electricity and Magnetism

- **Electric Circuits**: Understanding series and parallel circuits, Ohm's law ($V = IR$), and the relationship between voltage, current, and resistance.

- **Magnetism**: The relationship between electricity and magnetism, including electromagnetism and the behavior of magnetic fields.

Key Concepts in Chemistry

Chemistry is the study of matter, its properties, and the changes it undergoes. Here are the core topics you need to understand:

Properties of Matter

- **States of Matter**: Solid, liquid, gas, and plasma, and their characteristics.

- **Density**: The mass per unit volume of a substance, calculated using density = mass/volume.

- **Phase Changes**: Transitions between different states of matter, such as melting, boiling, and sublimation.

Chemical Reactions

- **Types of Reactions**: Synthesis, decomposition, single replacement, double replacement, and combustion.

- **Balancing Chemical Equations**: Ensuring the number of atoms of each element is the same on both sides of the equation.

- **Law of Conservation of Mass**: Mass is neither created nor destroyed in a chemical reaction.

Atomic Structure

- **Atoms and Molecules**: The basic building blocks of matter, consisting of protons, neutrons, and electrons.

- **Periodic Table**: The arrangement of elements based on their atomic number, and periodic trends such as electronegativity, atomic radius, and ionization energy.

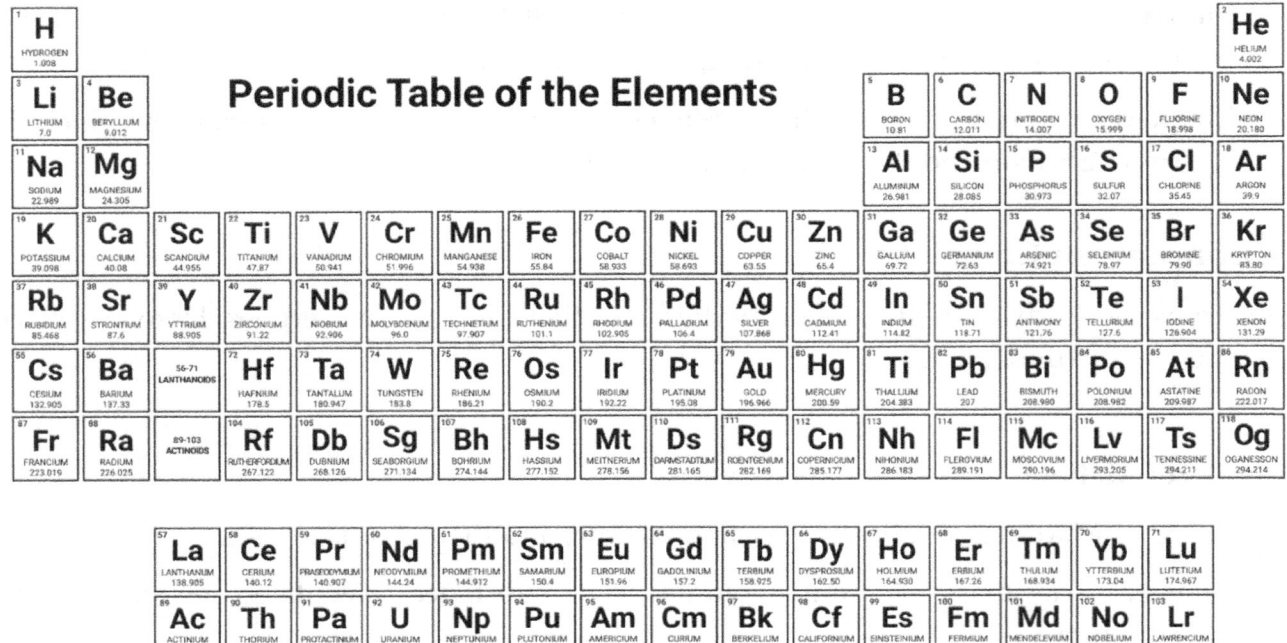

Chemical Bonding

- **Ionic Bonds**: Formed when electrons are transferred from one atom to another, creating ions.

- **Covalent Bonds**: Formed when atoms share electrons.

- **Metallic Bonds**: The attraction between free-floating valence electrons and positively charged metal ions.

Practical Applications

Understanding the principles of physics and chemistry is crucial for various practical applications:

Engineering

- **Structural Engineering**: Uses principles of physics to design and analyze structures, ensuring they can withstand forces and stresses.

- **Chemical Engineering**: Applies chemical principles to develop processes for manufacturing chemicals, pharmaceuticals, and materials.

Medicine

- **Pharmacology**: Chemistry is essential in the development and testing of new drugs.

- **Medical Imaging**: Physics principles are applied in techniques such as X-rays, MRI, and ultrasound.

Environmental Science

- **Pollution Control**: Chemistry helps in understanding pollutants and developing methods to reduce their impact.

- **Energy Resources**: Physics and chemistry are used to explore and develop renewable energy sources.

Practice Problems

To reinforce your understanding of physical science concepts, solve these practice problems:

1. **Physics - Force and Motion**: A 5 kg object is subjected to a net force of 20 N. Calculate its acceleration.

   o Solution: Use Newton's second law: $F = m * a$

   o $a = F/m = 20 \, N / 5 \, kg = 4 \, m/s^2$

2. **Chemistry - Balancing Equations**: Balance the chemical equation for the reaction between hydrogen and oxygen to form water: $H_2 + O_2 \rightarrow H_2O$.

   o Solution: Balanced equation: $2H_2 + O_2 \rightarrow 2H_2O$

3. **Physics - Energy**: Calculate the potential energy of a 10 kg object raised to a height of 5 meters.

   o Solution: Use the potential energy formula: $PE = m * g * h$

   o $PE = 10 \, kg * 9.8 \, m/s^2 * 5 \, m = 490$ Joules

4. **Chemistry - Periodic Table**: Identify the number of protons, neutrons, and electrons in a neutral atom of carbon-12 (C-12).

   o Solution: Carbon-12 has 6 protons, 6 neutrons, and 6 electrons.

By mastering these physical science concepts and practicing regularly, you will develop the skills needed to solve a wide range of scientific problems confidently and accurately. Next, we will explore Life Science: Biology, where you will learn to understand biological principles and their applications.

Life Science: Biology

Biology, the study of living organisms and their interactions with the environment, is a crucial component of the Science section of the GED test. This section will cover fundamental biological concepts, including cell structure and function, genetics, evolution, and ecosystems. Understanding these principles is essential for analyzing biological phenomena and solving related problems.

Key Concepts in Biology

Cell Structure and Function

- **Cell Theory**: The cell is the basic unit of life. All living organisms are composed of one or more cells, and all cells arise from pre-existing cells.

- **Types of Cells**: Eukaryotic cells (with a nucleus and membrane-bound organelles) and prokaryotic cells (without a nucleus).

- **Cell Organelles**: Key organelles include the nucleus (controls cell activities), mitochondria (produces energy), ribosomes (synthesizes proteins), endoplasmic reticulum (processes proteins and lipids), and chloroplasts (photosynthesis in plant cells).

- **Cell Membrane**: A phospholipid bilayer that controls the movement of substances in and out of the cell through passive (diffusion, osmosis) and active transport mechanisms.

PROKARYOTIC CELL

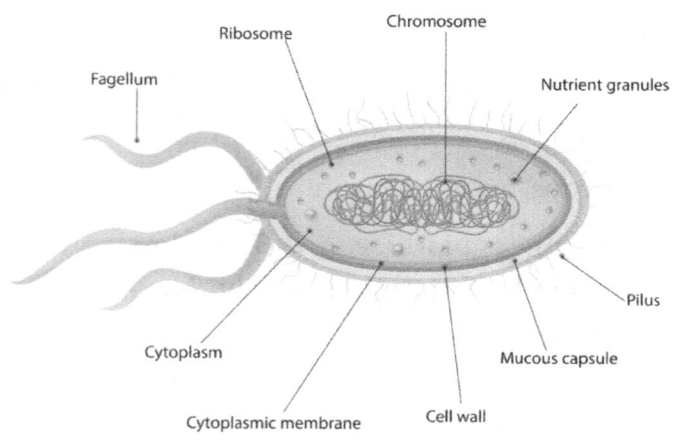

EUKARYOTIC CELL

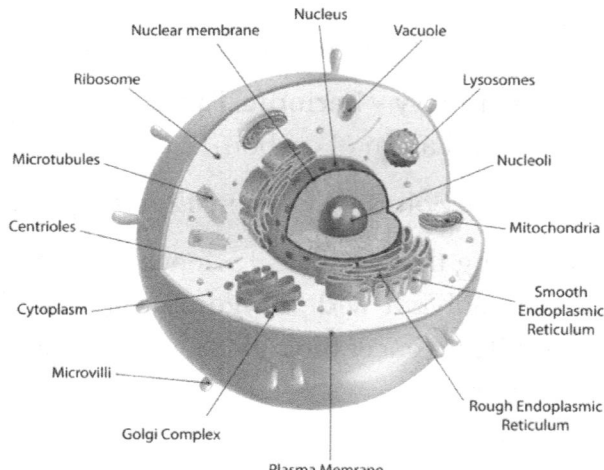

Genetics

- **DNA and RNA**: DNA (deoxyribonucleic acid) stores genetic information, while RNA (ribonucleic acid) helps in protein synthesis.

- **Genes and Chromosomes**: Genes are segments of DNA that code for proteins, and chromosomes are structures within cells that contain a person's genes.

- **Mendelian Genetics**: Gregor Mendel's principles of inheritance, including concepts of dominant and recessive alleles, genotype and phenotype, and Punnett squares to predict genetic outcomes.

- **Mutations**: Changes in the DNA sequence that can lead to genetic variation and potentially cause diseases.

Evolution

- **Natural Selection**: Charles Darwin's theory that organisms better adapted to their environment tend to survive and produce more offspring.

- **Speciation**: The formation of new and distinct species in the course of evolution.

- **Evidence of Evolution**: Fossil records, comparative anatomy, embryology, and molecular biology that support the theory of evolution.

Ecosystems

- **Biotic and Abiotic Factors**: Biotic factors are living components of an ecosystem (plants, animals, microorganisms), while abiotic factors are non-living components (water, sunlight, temperature).

- **Food Chains and Food Webs**: Models that show the flow of energy through an ecosystem, from producers (plants) to consumers (herbivores, carnivores) and decomposers (fungi, bacteria).

- **Ecological Relationships**: Interactions between organisms, including predation, competition, symbiosis (mutualism, commensalism, parasitism), and the impact of human activities on ecosystems.

Practical Applications

Understanding biological principles has numerous practical applications:

Medicine and Healthcare

- **Genetics**: Knowledge of genetics is crucial for understanding inherited diseases, genetic testing, and developing gene therapies.

- **Cell Biology**: Understanding cell function and pathology is essential for diagnosing and treating diseases at the cellular level.

- **Evolutionary Biology**: Insights into evolutionary processes help in understanding antibiotic resistance and developing new vaccines.

Environmental Science

- **Conservation Biology**: Applying ecological principles to protect endangered species and manage natural resources sustainably.

- **Ecosystem Management**: Understanding ecological interactions to restore and maintain healthy ecosystems.

Agriculture

- **Genetically Modified Organisms (GMOs)**: Using genetic engineering to enhance crop yields, pest resistance, and nutritional value.

- **Sustainable Farming Practices**: Applying ecological principles to develop sustainable agricultural methods that reduce environmental impact.

Practice Problems

To reinforce your understanding of biological concepts, solve these practice problems:

1. **Cell Structure**: Identify the function of the mitochondria in a eukaryotic cell.

   o Solution: The mitochondria produce energy in the form of ATP through cellular respiration.

2. **Genetics**: Use a Punnett square to predict the offspring of a cross between two heterozygous (Aa) individuals for a single trait.

   o Solution: The possible genotypes are AA, Aa, and aa, with a phenotypic ratio of 3:1 for the dominant trait.

3. **Evolution**: Explain the process of natural selection.

   o Solution: Natural selection is the process where organisms with favorable traits are more likely to survive and reproduce, passing those traits to the next generation.

4. **Ecosystems**: Describe the role of decomposers in a food web.

   o Solution: Decomposers break down dead organisms and recycle nutrients back into the ecosystem, supporting the growth of producers.

By mastering these biological concepts and practicing regularly, you will develop the skills needed to analyze and solve a wide range of biological problems confidently and accurately. Next, we will explore Earth and Space Science, where you will learn to understand geological and astronomical principles and their applications.

CHAPTER 5
SCIENCE

Earth and Space Science

Earth and Space Science explores the physical characteristics of our planet and the universe beyond. This section covers fundamental concepts in geology, meteorology, oceanography, and astronomy. Understanding these principles is essential for interpreting natural phenomena and solving related problems. Here, we will delve into the structure of the Earth, the dynamics of its atmosphere and oceans, and the vast expanse of space.

Key Concepts in Earth and Space Science

Geology

- **Layers of the Earth**: The Earth is composed of three main layers: the crust (outermost layer), the mantle (middle layer), and the core (innermost layer). The crust is further divided into continental and oceanic crust.

- **Plate Tectonics**: The Earth's lithosphere is divided into tectonic plates that move on the asthenosphere. Plate movements cause earthquakes, volcanic activity, and the formation of mountains.

- **Rock Cycle**: Describes the formation and transformation of rocks through processes like melting, cooling, erosion, and compression. There are three main types of rocks: igneous, sedimentary, and metamorphic.

- **Fossils and Geological Time**: Fossils provide evidence of past life and are used to understand the geological time scale, which divides Earth's history into eons, eras, periods, and epochs.

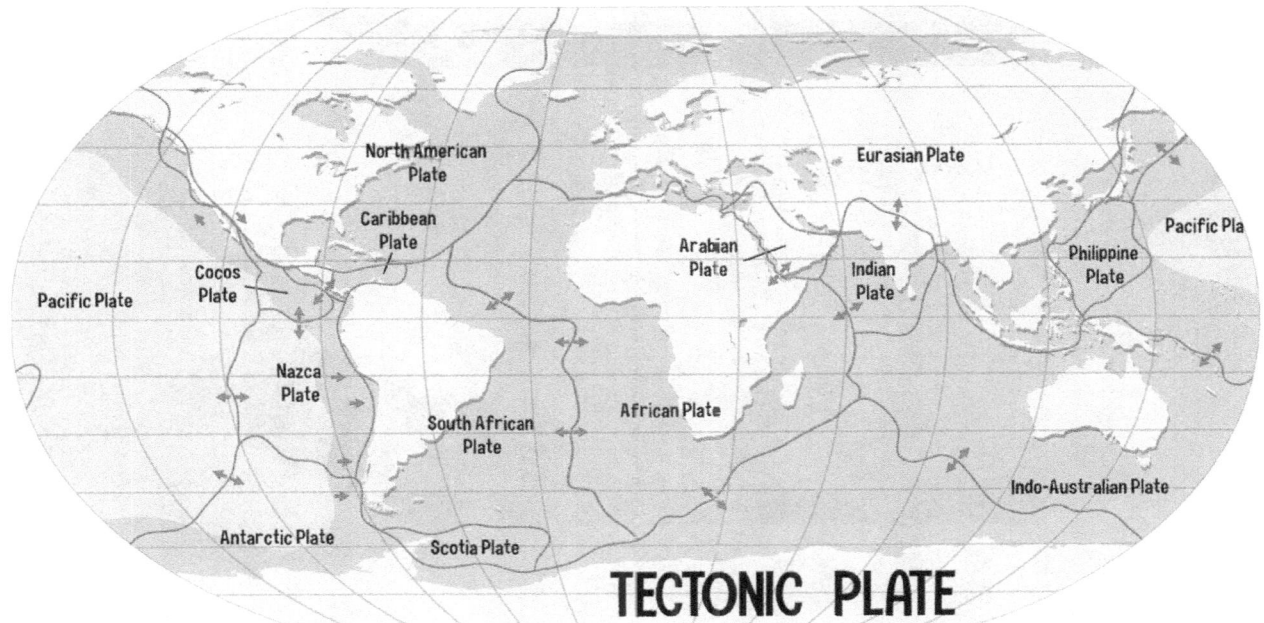

Meteorology

- **Atmospheric Layers**: The Earth's atmosphere is divided into layers based on temperature gradients: the troposphere (where weather occurs), stratosphere (contains the ozone layer), mesosphere, thermosphere, and exosphere.

- **Weather and Climate**: Weather refers to short-term atmospheric conditions, while climate describes long-term patterns. Key factors include temperature, humidity, precipitation, wind, and atmospheric pressure.

- **Weather Systems**: Includes high and low-pressure systems, fronts (boundary between air masses), and storm systems (such as hurricanes and tornadoes).

- **Climate Change**: Refers to long-term changes in temperature and weather patterns, primarily due to human activities like burning fossil fuels, deforestation, and industrial processes.

ATMOSPHERIC FRONT

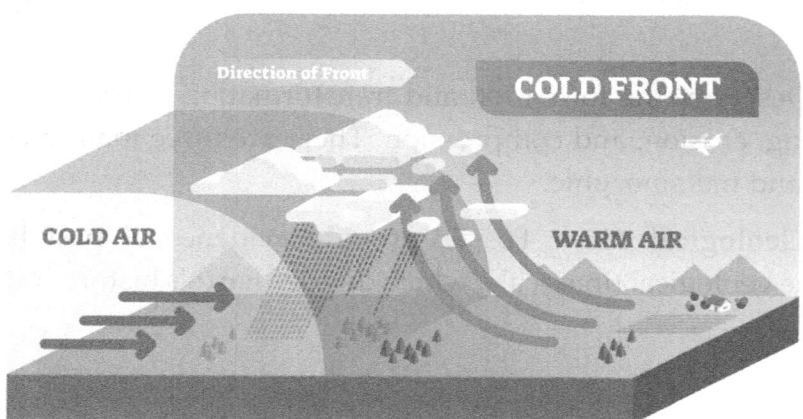

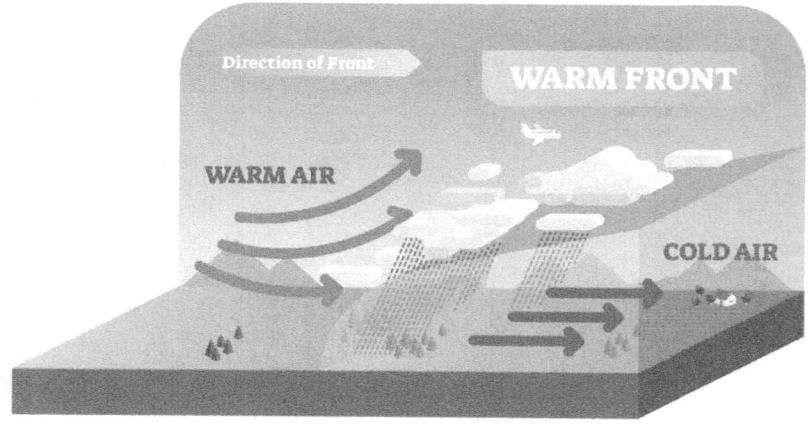

Oceanography

- **Ocean Layers**: The ocean is divided into layers based on depth and light penetration: the epipelagic (sunlight zone), mesopelagic (twilight zone), bathypelagic (midnight zone), abyssopelagic, and hadalpelagic zones.

- **Ocean Currents**: Ocean currents are large-scale movements of water that distribute heat around the planet. They are driven by wind, water density differences, and the Earth's rotation.

- **Tides and Waves**: Tides are caused by the gravitational pull of the moon and the sun, while waves are generated by wind.

- **Marine Ecosystems**: Includes coral reefs, deep-sea vents, and coastal environments, each supporting diverse life forms.

Astronomy

- **Solar System**: Comprises the sun, eight planets, moons, dwarf planets, and other celestial objects like asteroids and comets. Understanding the orbits and characteristics of these objects is fundamental.

- **Stars and Galaxies**: Stars are massive celestial bodies that emit light and heat. Galaxies are vast collections of stars, gas, dust, and dark matter. The Milky Way is our home galaxy.

- **Cosmology**: The study of the origin, evolution, and eventual fate of the universe. Key concepts include the Big Bang Theory, cosmic microwave background radiation, and dark matter/energy.

- **Space Exploration**: Human and robotic exploration of space, including missions to the moon, Mars, and beyond. Technological advancements have expanded our understanding of the universe.

Practical Applications

Understanding Earth and Space Science has numerous practical applications:

Environmental Science

- **Natural Disaster Preparedness**: Knowledge of geological and meteorological processes helps in predicting and preparing for natural disasters like earthquakes, tsunamis, and hurricanes.

- **Climate Mitigation**: Understanding climate change is crucial for developing strategies to reduce greenhouse gas emissions and adapt to changing climate conditions.

Astronomy and Space Exploration

- **Technological Innovation**: Space exploration drives technological advancements in fields like telecommunications, GPS, and materials science.

- **Scientific Research**: Studying celestial bodies and cosmic phenomena enhances our understanding of fundamental physics and the origins of the universe.

Marine Science

- **Sustainable Fisheries**: Knowledge of marine ecosystems helps in managing fisheries sustainably to prevent overfishing and protect marine biodiversity.

- **Ocean Conservation**: Understanding ocean currents and ecosystems is vital for addressing issues like plastic pollution and coral reef degradation.

Practice Problems

To reinforce your understanding of Earth and Space Science concepts, solve these practice problems:

1. **Geology**: Explain the process of plate tectonics and how it leads to the formation of mountains.

   o Solution: Plate tectonics involves the movement of the Earth's lithospheric plates. When two plates collide, they can push up the crust to form mountains, such as the Himalayas.

2. **Meteorology**: Describe the differences between weather and climate.

   o Solution: Weather refers to short-term atmospheric conditions like temperature and precipitation, while climate describes long-term patterns and averages of weather in a specific region.

3. **Oceanography**: Explain how ocean currents affect global climate.

   o Solution: Ocean currents distribute heat around the planet, influencing climate patterns. For example, the Gulf Stream warms the climate of Western Europe.

4. **Astronomy**: Describe the Big Bang Theory.

   o Solution: The Big Bang Theory posits that the universe began as a singularity approximately 13.8 billion years ago and has been expanding ever since. Evidence includes the cosmic microwave background radiation and the observed redshift of galaxies.

By mastering these Earth and Space Science concepts and practicing regularly, you will develop the skills needed to analyze and solve a wide range of scientific problems confidently and accurately. Next, we will explore Sample Questions and Answer Explanations, where you will practice applying these skills in a test-like environment and learn from detailed explanations.

Sample Questions and Answer Explanations

Practicing with sample questions and understanding their explanations is an essential part of preparing for the Science section of the GED test. This approach helps you familiarize yourself with the types of questions you will encounter, improve your problem-solving skills, and build confidence. In this section, we provide a variety of sample questions from each scientific domain, followed by detailed explanations of the answers, to help you master the concepts covered in this chapter.

Sample Question 1: Geology

Question: What is the primary cause of earthquakes?

A. Erosion B. Volcanic activity C. Movement of tectonic plates D. Weathering of rocks

Answer: C. Movement of tectonic plates

Explanation: Earthquakes are primarily caused by the movement of tectonic plates. When these plates grind against each other or collide, the stress is released in the form of seismic waves, causing the ground to shake. Erosion and weathering are slow processes that break down rocks but do not cause sudden seismic activity.

Sample Question 2: Meteorology

Question: Which layer of the atmosphere contains the ozone layer?

A. Troposphere B. Stratosphere C. Mesosphere D. Thermosphere

Answer: B. Stratosphere

Explanation: The stratosphere contains the ozone layer, which absorbs most of the sun's harmful ultraviolet radiation. The troposphere is the layer where weather occurs, the mesosphere is where meteors burn up, and the thermosphere is the uppermost layer, where the auroras occur.

Sample Question 3: Oceanography

Question: What drives the movement of deep ocean currents?

A. Wind patterns B. Salinity and temperature differences C. Earth's rotation D. Tidal forces

Answer: B. Salinity and temperature differences

Explanation: Deep ocean currents are driven primarily by differences in salinity and temperature, a process known as thermohaline circulation. Wind patterns primarily drive surface currents, while tidal forces affect the rise and fall of sea levels.

Sample Question 4: Astronomy

Question: Which planet is known for its extensive ring system?

A. Mars B. Jupiter C. Saturn D. Neptune

Answer: C. Saturn

Explanation: Saturn is known for its extensive and prominent ring system, which is composed of ice and rock particles. While Jupiter, Uranus, and Neptune also have ring systems, they are less prominent and extensive compared to Saturn's.

Sample Question 5: Biology

Question: Which organelle is responsible for producing energy in the form of ATP in eukaryotic cells?

A. Nucleus B. Ribosome C. Mitochondrion D. Endoplasmic reticulum

Answer: C. Mitochondrion

Explanation: The mitochondrion is known as the powerhouse of the cell because it produces energy in the form of ATP through cellular respiration. The nucleus contains genetic material, ribosomes are involved in protein synthesis, and the endoplasmic reticulum processes proteins and lipids.

Sample Question 6: Genetics

Question: In Mendelian genetics, what is the expected phenotypic ratio of a monohybrid cross between two heterozygous individuals (Aa)?

A. 1:2:1 B. 3:1 C. 9:3:3:1 D. 1:1

Answer: B. 3:1

Explanation: A monohybrid cross between two heterozygous individuals (Aa) typically results in a phenotypic ratio of 3:1, where three offspring display the dominant trait and one displays the recessive trait. The 1:2:1 ratio refers to genotypic ratio, and 9:3:3:1 is the phenotypic ratio for a dihybrid cross.

Sample Question 7: Ecology

Question: What role do decomposers play in an ecosystem?

A. Producing energy through photosynthesis B. Consuming primary producers C. Breaking down dead organisms and recycling nutrients D. Competing with other organisms for resources

Answer: C. Breaking down dead organisms and recycling nutrients

Explanation: Decomposers, such as bacteria and fungi, play a crucial role in breaking down dead organisms and recycling nutrients back into the ecosystem. This process is essential for maintaining the flow of nutrients and supporting the growth of producers.

Sample Question 8: Earth Science

Question: Which geological process is responsible for the formation of the Grand Canyon?

A. Volcanic activity B. Plate tectonics C. Erosion by water D. Deposition of sediments

Answer: C. Erosion by water

Explanation: The Grand Canyon was primarily formed by the erosion caused by the Colorado River over millions of years. This process carved out the deep canyon, exposing layers of rock and creating the landscape we see today.

Sample Question 9: Chemistry

Question: What is the balanced chemical equation for the reaction between hydrogen (H_2) and oxygen (O_2) to form water (H_2O)?

A. $H_2 + O_2 \rightarrow H_2O$ B. $2H_2 + O_2 \rightarrow 2H_2O$ C. $H_2 + 2O_2 \rightarrow H_2O_2$ D. $2H_2 + 2O_2 \rightarrow 2H_2O_2$

Answer: B. $2H_2 + O_2 \rightarrow 2H_2O$

Explanation: The balanced chemical equation for the reaction between hydrogen and oxygen to form water is $2H_2 + O_2 \rightarrow 2H_2O$. Balancing chemical equations ensures that the same number of atoms of each element is present on both sides of the equation.

Sample Question 10: Physics

Question: Calculate the kinetic energy of a 2 kg object moving at a velocity of 3 m/s.

A. 3 Joules B. 6 Joules C. 9 Joules D. 18 Joules

Answer: C. 9 Joules

Explanation: The kinetic energy (KE) of an object is calculated using the formula $KE = (1/2) * m * v^2$. Substituting the given values: $KE = 0.5 * 2 \text{ kg} * (3 \text{ m/s})^2 = 0.5 * 2 * 9 = 9$ Joules.

By practicing these sample questions and thoroughly understanding the explanations, you will strengthen your scientific reasoning skills and be better prepared for the GED test. Regular practice with a variety of problems helps solidify your understanding and improves your ability to apply scientific concepts effectively. Next, we will explore Interpreting Graphs and Tables, where you will learn to analyze and draw conclusions from various types of data presentations.

Interpreting Graphs and Tables

Interpreting graphs and tables is a critical skill in the Science section of the GED test. These visual tools help convey complex data in an understandable format, allowing you to analyze trends, make comparisons, and draw conclusions. In this section, we will explore different types of graphs and tables, provide strategies for interpreting them, and offer practice examples to enhance your skills.

Types of Graphs and Tables

Line Graphs

- **Usage**: Line graphs are used to display data points over a continuous period. They are particularly useful for showing trends over time.

- **Components**: Include a horizontal axis (x-axis) representing time or another continuous variable, and a vertical axis (y-axis) representing the variable being measured.

- **Interpretation**: Look for trends, such as upward or downward slopes, and note any peaks or troughs.

Bar Graphs

- **Usage**: Bar graphs are used to compare quantities across different categories. Each bar represents a category, with the height or length of the bar indicating the quantity.

- **Components**: Comprise a horizontal axis (x-axis) representing categories and a vertical axis (y-axis) representing quantities.

- **Interpretation**: Compare the heights or lengths of the bars to understand the relative sizes of the categories.

Pie Charts

- **Usage**: Pie charts show the proportions of a whole. Each slice represents a category, with the size of the slice indicating its proportion relative to the whole.

- **Components**: A circular chart divided into slices, each labeled with the category it represents.

- **Interpretation**: Examine the size of each slice to understand the proportion of each category.

Tables

- **Usage**: Tables organize data into rows and columns, making it easy to read and compare values.

- **Components**: Include headers for each column and row, providing labels for the data presented.

- **Interpretation**: Read across rows and down columns to find specific data points and make comparisons.

Scatter Plots

- **Usage**: Scatter plots display data points on a Cartesian plane, showing the relationship between two variables.

- **Components**: Include an x-axis and a y-axis, with each point representing a pair of values.

- **Interpretation**: Look for patterns, such as clusters, trends, or correlations between variables.

Strategies for Interpreting Graphs and Tables

1. **Read Titles and Labels**: Always start by reading the title, axis labels, and any legends or keys. This information provides context and helps you understand what the graph or table represents.

2. **Identify Units of Measurement**: Pay attention to the units of measurement used on the axes or in the table. Understanding the units is crucial for accurate interpretation.

3. **Analyze Trends and Patterns**: Look for overall trends, patterns, and anomalies in the data. Note any significant increases, decreases, or stable periods.

4. **Compare Data Points**: Make comparisons between different data points or categories. Determine which values are highest, lowest, or equal.

5. **Examine Scales and Intervals**: Check the scales and intervals on the axes. Uneven intervals can sometimes mislead interpretation, so ensure you understand the scale being used.

6. **Look for Outliers**: Identify any data points that deviate significantly from the rest. Outliers can indicate errors, special cases, or important phenomena.

Practice Examples

Example 1: Line Graph Interpretation

A line graph shows the temperature over a week.

- **Title**: Temperature Over a Week
- **X-Axis**: Days (Monday to Sunday)
- **Y-Axis**: Temperature (°C)

Questions:

1. What is the trend in temperature from Monday to Wednesday?
2. On which day was the highest temperature recorded?
3. Describe any significant changes in temperature over the week.

Answers:

1. The temperature increases from Monday to Wednesday.
2. The highest temperature was recorded on Friday.
3. There was a significant drop in temperature on Thursday, followed by a peak on Friday and a gradual decrease towards the weekend.

Example 2: Bar Graph Interpretation

A bar graph compares the sales of four products in a month.

- **Title**: Monthly Sales of Products
- **X-Axis**: Products (A, B, C, D)
- **Y-Axis**: Sales (units)

Questions:

1. Which product had the highest sales?
2. How do the sales of Product C compare to Product A?
3. Identify any products with similar sales figures.

Answers:

1. Product B had the highest sales.
2. Product C had lower sales than Product A.
3. Products C and D had similar sales figures.

Example 3: Table Interpretation

A table shows the population of different cities in a country.

City	Population (2020)	Population (2021)
City A	1,000,000	1,050,000
City B	500,000	520,000
City C	750,000	740,000

Questions:

1. Which city had the highest population growth between 2020 and 2021?
2. Did any city experience a population decrease?
3. Compare the populations of City A and City B in 2021.

Answers:

1. City A had the highest population growth (50,000 increase).
2. City C experienced a population decrease (10,000 decrease).
3. In 2021, City A's population (1,050,000) was significantly higher than City B's population (520,000).

Example 4: Pie Chart Interpretation

A pie chart shows the market share of different smartphone brands.

- **Title**: Market Share of Smartphone Brands
- **Categories**: Brand A, Brand B, Brand C, Brand D

Questions:

1. Which brand has the largest market share?
2. How does Brand C's market share compare to Brand A's?
3. What can you infer about the competition among these brands?

Answers:

1. Brand A has the largest market share.
2. Brand C's market share is smaller than Brand A's.
3. The market is competitive, with Brand A leading, but other brands also holding significant shares.

CHAPTER 6
SOCIAL STUDIES

The Social Studies section of the GED test assesses your understanding of history, geography, civics, government, and economics. This section not only tests your knowledge of facts but also your ability to analyze and interpret historical documents, data, and other information sources. Mastering these subjects is essential for developing a well-rounded perspective on societal structures and historical events. This chapter provides a comprehensive overview of each topic, offering detailed explanations, practical examples, and strategies to help you succeed.

Section Overview

The Social Studies section is designed to evaluate your ability to understand and analyze social studies concepts and information. This includes interpreting historical events, understanding governmental and economic systems, and analyzing geographical data. Here's an overview of what to expect in this section:

Test Structure and Timing

- **Duration**: The Social Studies section is 70 minutes long.

- **Question Types**: The section includes multiple-choice, drag-and-drop, drop-down, fill-in-the-blank, and hot spot questions. These questions test your ability to interpret texts, analyze graphs and charts, and apply social studies concepts.

- **Scoring**: Each question in the Social Studies section contributes to your overall score, which ranges from 100 to 200. A passing score of 145 is required.

Skills Assessed

The Social Studies section evaluates several key skills, including:

- **Reading Comprehension**: Understanding and interpreting written texts, including primary and secondary sources.

- **Analysis and Interpretation**: Analyzing historical events, government structures, economic principles, and geographical data.

- **Critical Thinking**: Applying social studies concepts to real-world scenarios and drawing conclusions based on evidence.

- **Data Analysis**: Interpreting graphs, charts, tables, and maps to understand social studies phenomena.

Preparation Tips

To prepare effectively for the Social Studies section, it's important to develop a systematic approach to studying and practicing:

1. **Review Key Concepts**: Ensure you have a solid understanding of fundamental concepts in U.S. history, world history, geography, civics, government, and economics.

2. **Practice Data Interpretation**: Regularly practice interpreting data from graphs, tables, and maps. This skill is crucial for answering many questions in the Social Studies section.

3. **Utilize Resources**: Take advantage of study guides, online tutorials, and educational videos to reinforce your learning. The explanations and examples in this book will also help clarify complex topics.

4. **Take Practice Tests**: Complete full-length practice tests under timed conditions to build confidence and improve your test-taking skills. Reviewing your answers and understanding any mistakes is essential for improvement.

By understanding the structure and requirements of the Social Studies section, you can approach your preparation with confidence and focus. Let's delve deeper into each major area, starting with U.S. History.

U.S. History

U.S. History encompasses the significant events, movements, and figures that have shaped the United States from its founding to the present day. Understanding these historical milestones is crucial for analyzing the development of American society and its role in the world.

Key Topics in U.S. History

- **Colonial America**: The establishment of the thirteen colonies, colonial life, and interactions with Native Americans.

- **American Revolution**: Causes, major battles, key figures, and the outcomes of the war for independence.

- **Constitution and Early Republic**: The drafting of the Constitution, Federalist and Anti-Federalist debates, the Bill of Rights, and the early years of the republic.

- **Civil War and Reconstruction**: Causes of the Civil War, key events and battles, the Emancipation Proclamation, Reconstruction policies, and their impact.

- **Industrialization and Progressivism**: The rise of industrial America, labor movements, and Progressive Era reforms.

- **World Wars I and II**: Causes, major events, and the impact of the world wars on American society and global politics.

- **Civil Rights Movement**: Key events, figures, and legislation that advanced civil rights in the United States.

- **Contemporary America**: Recent political, social, and economic developments, including technological advancements and current issues.

Practical Applications

Understanding U.S. history helps you gain insights into the country's political and social dynamics, fostering informed citizenship and critical thinking about current events.

Practice Problems

To reinforce your understanding of U.S. history concepts, solve these practice problems:

1. **Colonial America**: Describe the economic activities of the New England colonies.

   o Solution: The New England colonies were primarily involved in fishing, shipbuilding, and trade due to their coastal geography and natural resources.

2. **American Revolution**: Identify the significance of the Battle of Saratoga.

   o Solution: The Battle of Saratoga was a turning point in the American Revolution because it resulted in a decisive American victory and convinced France to join the war as an ally to the United States.

3. **Constitution**: Explain the main purpose of the Bill of Rights.

   o Solution: The Bill of Rights was added to the Constitution to protect individual liberties and limit the power of the federal government by guaranteeing fundamental rights such as freedom of speech, religion, and the press.

By mastering these U.S. history concepts and practicing regularly, you will develop the skills needed to analyze and interpret historical events confidently and accurately. Next, we will explore World History, where you will learn to understand global historical developments and their impacts.

U.S. History

U.S. History covers the major events, movements, and figures that have shaped the United States from its inception to the present day. A thorough understanding of these historical milestones is essential for analyzing the development of American society and its role on the global stage. This section will delve into key periods and themes in U.S. history, providing comprehensive insights and practical examples to enhance your understanding.

Colonial America

The history of the United States begins with the establishment of the thirteen colonies. These colonies were founded primarily by English settlers, but also included Dutch, Swedish, and other European groups. The economic activities in the colonies were diverse and region-specific:

- **New England Colonies**: Characterized by small farms, fishing, shipbuilding, and trade. The economy was less reliant on slavery compared to the southern colonies.

- **Middle Colonies**: Known as the "breadbasket" for their large grain production. They had diverse economies, including farming, mining, and manufacturing.

- **Southern Colonies**: Dependent on plantation agriculture, growing cash crops like tobacco, rice, and indigo. The economy heavily relied on enslaved labor.

The interactions between European settlers and Native Americans varied, ranging from trade and cooperation to conflict and displacement. These early interactions set the stage for future relations and expansion.

American Revolution

The American Revolution was a pivotal moment in U.S. history, resulting in independence from British rule. Key events and concepts include:

- **Causes**: Tensions arose from British policies like the Stamp Act, Townshend Acts, and the Intolerable Acts, which imposed taxes and regulations on the colonies without representation in Parliament.

- **Major Battles**: Significant battles included Lexington and Concord, Bunker Hill, Saratoga, and Yorktown. The Battle of Saratoga was especially crucial as it secured French support for the American cause.

- **Key Figures**: Leaders such as George Washington, Thomas Jefferson, Benjamin Franklin, and John Adams played vital roles in the revolution and the formation of the new nation.

- **Outcomes**: The Treaty of Paris (1783) officially ended the war, recognizing American independence and granting significant territorial gains to the United States.

Constitution and Early Republic

The post-revolution period involved establishing a stable government and addressing internal and external challenges:

- **Drafting the Constitution**: The Articles of Confederation proved inadequate, leading to the Constitutional Convention in 1787. The resulting U.S. Constitution established a federal system with checks and balances among three branches of government.

- **Federalist vs. Anti-Federalist Debate**: Federalists supported a strong central government, while Anti-Federalists advocated for states' rights and individual liberties. This debate led to the inclusion of the Bill of Rights to protect individual freedoms.

- **Early Presidencies**: The administrations of George Washington, John Adams, and Thomas Jefferson set precedents for future governance and addressed issues like national debt, foreign policy, and domestic stability.

Civil War and Reconstruction

The Civil War was a defining conflict that addressed the issues of slavery and states' rights, leading to significant social and political changes:

- **Causes**: Key causes included the expansion of slavery into new territories, states' rights, and economic differences between the North and South.

- **Major Events**: Key battles and events included Fort Sumter, Antietam, Gettysburg, and Sherman's March to the Sea. The Emancipation Proclamation (1863) declared the freedom of slaves in Confederate states.

- **Reconstruction**: The post-war period focused on rebuilding the South and integrating freed slaves into society. Key amendments during this time were the 13th (abolishing slavery), 14th (granting citizenship), and 15th (granting voting rights to African American men).

Industrialization and Progressivism

The late 19th and early 20th centuries saw significant economic and social changes:

- **Industrial Growth**: The rise of factories, railroads, and technological innovations transformed the economy. Key figures included industrialists like Andrew Carnegie and John D. Rockefeller.

- **Labor Movements**: Workers organized to demand better wages, hours, and conditions, leading to strikes and the formation of labor unions.

- **Progressive Era**: Reformers aimed to address the social issues caused by industrialization. Key reforms included antitrust laws, labor protections, and women's suffrage (19th Amendment).

World Wars I and II

The world wars had profound impacts on American society and its global role:

- **World War I**: The U.S. entered the war in 1917, contributing to the Allied victory. The war led to significant social changes, including the Great Migration of African Americans to northern cities.

- **World War II**: The attack on Pearl Harbor in 1941 brought the U.S. into the war. Key events included D-Day, the Battle of Midway, and the dropping of atomic bombs on Hiroshima and Nagasaki. The war ended with the Allied victory in 1945.

Civil Rights Movement

The mid-20th century saw significant strides in civil rights for African Americans and other marginalized groups:

- **Key Events**: The Brown v. Board of Education (1954) decision, the Montgomery Bus Boycott (1955-1956), and the March on Washington (1963) were pivotal moments.

- **Key Figures**: Leaders like Martin Luther King Jr., Malcolm X, Rosa Parks, and Thurgood Marshall played crucial roles.

- **Legislation**: The Civil Rights Act of 1964 and the Voting Rights Act of 1965 were landmark laws that aimed to end segregation and protect voting rights.

Contemporary America

Recent history has been shaped by technological advancements, political changes, and social movements:

- **Technological Advancements**: Innovations in computers, the internet, and biotechnology have transformed everyday life and the economy.

- **Political Changes**: The end of the Cold War, the rise of globalization, and recent political polarization have impacted domestic and foreign policy.

- **Social Movements**: Movements for LGBTQ+ rights, climate action, and racial justice continue to shape American society.

Practical Applications

Understanding U.S. history is essential for informed citizenship and critical analysis of current events. It provides context for understanding societal changes and governmental actions.

Practice Problems

To reinforce your understanding of U.S. history concepts, solve these practice problems:

1. **Colonial America**: Describe the economic activities of the Southern colonies.

   o Solution: The Southern colonies relied on plantation agriculture, growing cash crops like tobacco, rice, and indigo, and heavily used enslaved labor.

2. **American Revolution**: Explain the significance of the Declaration of Independence.

   o Solution: The Declaration of Independence, adopted on July 4, 1776, declared the American colonies' independence from Britain and outlined the principles of individual rights and government by consent.

3. **Civil War**: Identify the impact of the Emancipation Proclamation.

   o Solution: The Emancipation Proclamation, issued by President Lincoln in 1863, declared all slaves in Confederate-held territory free, shifting the war's focus to the abolition of slavery and allowing African Americans to join the Union Army.

By mastering these U.S. history concepts and practicing regularly, you will develop the skills needed to analyze and interpret historical events confidently and accurately.

World History

World History encompasses the study of major events, cultures, and movements that have shaped human civilization. Understanding these global historical developments provides insight into the interconnectedness of societies and the complexities of the modern world. This section will cover significant periods and themes in world history, offering comprehensive explanations and practical examples to enhance your understanding.

Ancient Civilizations

Ancient civilizations laid the foundation for modern societies through their innovations in governance, culture, and technology. Key civilizations include:

- **Mesopotamia**: Often called the "cradle of civilization," Mesopotamia saw the rise of the Sumerians, Akkadians, Babylonians, and Assyrians. Innovations included the development of writing (cuneiform), the wheel, and early legal codes such as the Code of Hammurabi.

- **Egypt**: Known for its monumental architecture, such as the pyramids, and its advancements in mathematics, medicine, and engineering. The civilization was centered around the Nile River, which provided fertile land for agriculture.

- **Indus Valley**: Notable for its urban planning, including well-organized cities like Harappa and Mohenjo-Daro, and its undeciphered script. The civilization thrived along the Indus River in present-day Pakistan and northwest India.

- **China**: Early Chinese civilizations, such as the Shang and Zhou dynasties, contributed to the development of writing, philosophy (Confucianism and Taoism), and significant technological advancements like silk production and metallurgy.

- **Greece and Rome**: Greek civilization influenced Western culture through its advancements in philosophy, science, and democracy. The Roman Empire expanded upon Greek ideas, creating a vast empire known for its legal system, engineering feats, and the spread of Christianity.

Middle Ages and Renaissance

The Middle Ages, followed by the Renaissance, were periods of significant transformation in Europe and beyond:

- **Middle Ages**: Characterized by feudalism, the rise of the Catholic Church, and frequent conflicts like the Crusades. Despite being termed the "Dark Ages," this period saw developments in agriculture, architecture (Gothic cathedrals), and the foundation of universities.

- **Renaissance**: A cultural and intellectual revival that began in Italy in the 14th century and spread across Europe. Key figures included Leonardo da Vinci, Michelangelo, and Galileo. The Renaissance emphasized humanism, art, science, and the rediscovery of classical knowledge.

Age of Exploration

The Age of Exploration in the 15th and 16th centuries led to the discovery of new lands and the establishment of global trade networks:

- **Explorers**: Figures such as Christopher Columbus, Vasco da Gama, and Ferdinand Magellan undertook voyages that expanded European knowledge of the world.

- **Colonization**: European powers, including Spain, Portugal, England, and France, established colonies in the Americas, Africa, and Asia. This era led to significant cultural exchanges but also to exploitation and the transatlantic slave trade.

Enlightenment and Revolutions

The Enlightenment of the 17th and 18th centuries fostered new ideas about government, society, and human rights, leading to significant political revolutions:

- **Enlightenment Thinkers**: Philosophers like John Locke, Voltaire, and Jean-Jacques Rousseau advocated for reason, individual rights, and the separation of church and state.

- **American Revolution**: Influenced by Enlightenment ideas, the American colonies declared independence from Britain in 1776, leading to the creation of the United States.

- **French Revolution**: Starting in 1789, the French Revolution sought to overthrow the monarchy and establish a republic based on liberty, equality, and fraternity. It led to significant social and political upheaval.

Industrial Revolution

The Industrial Revolution, beginning in the late 18th century, transformed economies and societies through technological advancements:

- **Technological Innovations**: Inventions such as the steam engine, spinning jenny, and power loom revolutionized manufacturing and transportation.

- **Urbanization**: The rise of factories led to the growth of cities and significant changes in living and working conditions.

- **Economic Changes**: Capitalism became the dominant economic system, leading to increased production, trade, and the rise of industrial tycoons.

World Wars and 20th Century Conflicts

The 20th century was marked by two world wars and numerous conflicts that reshaped global politics:

- **World War I**: Triggered by the assassination of Archduke Franz Ferdinand in 1914, the war involved major powers and led to significant loss of life and political changes. The Treaty of Versailles ended the war but imposed harsh penalties on Germany.

- **World War II**: Beginning in 1939 with the invasion of Poland by Nazi Germany, the war expanded to include major global powers. Key events included the Holocaust, the use of atomic bombs on Hiroshima and Nagasaki, and the eventual Allied victory in 1945.

- **Cold War**: A period of geopolitical tension between the United States and the Soviet Union, marked by ideological conflicts, nuclear arms race, and proxy wars in Korea, Vietnam, and elsewhere.

Decolonization and Modern Era

The latter half of the 20th century saw the end of colonial empires and the emergence of new nations:

- **Decolonization**: Former colonies in Africa, Asia, and the Caribbean gained independence, leading to the formation of new nations and significant political changes.

- **Globalization**: Advances in technology, communication, and transportation fostered greater global interconnectedness, impacting economies, cultures, and politics.

Practical Applications

Understanding world history is essential for comprehending current global issues, fostering cross-cultural understanding, and developing informed perspectives on international relations and historical contexts.

Practice Problems

To reinforce your understanding of world history concepts, solve these practice problems:

1. **Ancient Civilizations**: Describe the significance of the Code of Hammurabi.

   o Solution: The Code of Hammurabi was one of the earliest written legal codes, establishing laws and punishments to maintain order in Babylonian society.

2. **Renaissance**: Identify the contributions of Leonardo da Vinci to the Renaissance.

   o Solution: Leonardo da Vinci was a polymath who made significant contributions to art (e.g., Mona Lisa, The Last Supper), science (anatomical studies), and engineering (designs for various inventions).

3. **Industrial Revolution**: Explain the impact of the steam engine on industrialization.

   o Solution: The steam engine, invented by James Watt, revolutionized transportation and manufacturing by providing a reliable and powerful source of energy, leading to increased production and economic growth.

4. **World War II**: Describe the significance of D-Day.

   o Solution: D-Day (June 6, 1944) was the Allied invasion of Normandy, France, marking a turning point in World War II by establishing a Western front against Nazi Germany, leading to the liberation of occupied Europe.

Geography

Geography is the study of the Earth's landscapes, environments, and the relationships between people and their environments. It encompasses both physical geography, which examines natural features and processes, and human geography, which explores the spatial aspects of human existence. Understanding geography is essential for analyzing how natural and human systems interact and how these interactions shape the world. This section will provide a comprehensive overview of key geographical concepts, including physical features, human-environment interactions, and geographical skills.

Key Concepts in Geography

Physical Geography

Physical geography focuses on the natural features and processes of the Earth. Key topics include:

- **Landforms**: Understanding different types of landforms such as mountains, valleys, plateaus, plains, and deserts. These features are shaped by geological processes such as tectonic activity, erosion, and sedimentation.

  - **Mountains**: Formed by tectonic forces or volcanism. Examples include the Himalayas and the Andes.

  - **Rivers and Lakes**: Bodies of water that play crucial roles in ecosystems and human societies. Major rivers include the Nile, Amazon, and Mississippi.

  - **Deserts**: Arid regions with limited precipitation. Notable deserts include the Sahara and the Gobi.

  - **Oceans**: The vast bodies of saltwater covering about 71% of the Earth's surface, including the Pacific, Atlantic, Indian, Southern, and Arctic Oceans.

- **Climate and Weather**: Climate refers to long-term patterns of temperature and precipitation, while weather describes short-term atmospheric conditions.

  - **Climate Zones**: The Earth is divided into different climate zones, such as tropical, temperate, and polar, based on latitude and prevailing weather patterns.

  - **Weather Patterns**: Influenced by factors like latitude, altitude, and proximity to water bodies. Understanding weather phenomena such as hurricanes, tornadoes, and monsoons is crucial.

- **Ecosystems and Biomes**: Ecosystems are communities of living organisms interacting with their physical environment. Biomes are larger ecological units classified by dominant vegetation and climate.

  - **Tropical Rainforests**: Characterized by high biodiversity and rainfall.

- o **Grasslands**: Dominated by grasses, with temperate and tropical variations.
- o **Tundra**: Cold, treeless regions with permafrost.

Human Geography

Human geography examines the spatial aspects of human activities and their impact on the environment. Key topics include:

- **Population and Migration**: Studies the distribution, density, and growth of human populations, as well as migration patterns and their causes.
  - o **Population Density**: The number of people per unit area. High-density areas include cities, while low-density areas are rural or remote regions.
  - o **Migration**: The movement of people from one place to another, driven by factors such as economic opportunities, conflict, and environmental conditions.
- **Urbanization**: The growth of cities and the movement of people from rural to urban areas.
  - o **Urban Sprawl**: The uncontrolled expansion of urban areas into surrounding regions.
  - o **Sustainable Cities**: Focuses on creating urban environments that are environmentally friendly, economically viable, and socially inclusive.
- **Cultural Geography**: Explores the spatial distribution of cultural practices, languages, religions, and ethnicities.
  - o **Cultural Landscapes**: Areas modified by human activity, reflecting cultural beliefs and practices.
  - o **Globalization**: The increasing interconnectedness of cultures and economies, leading to the exchange of goods, ideas, and practices.
- **Economic Geography**: Studies the spatial distribution of economic activities, including agriculture, industry, and services.
  - o **Agricultural Patterns**: The distribution of different types of agriculture based on climate, soil, and cultural practices.
  - o **Industrial Regions**: Areas with a high concentration of manufacturing activities, such as the Rust Belt in the United States.
  - o **Global Trade**: The exchange of goods and services between countries, influenced by factors like resource availability and trade policies.

Geographical Skills

Developing geographical skills is essential for interpreting and analyzing spatial data. Key skills include:

- **Map Reading and Interpretation**: Understanding different types of maps, such as political, physical, and thematic maps. Key elements include scale, legend, and compass rose.

    o **Topographic Maps**: Show elevation and landforms using contour lines.

    o **Thematic Maps**: Focus on specific themes, such as population density or climate.

- **Geospatial Technologies**: The use of tools like Geographic Information Systems (GIS), remote sensing, and Global Positioning Systems (GPS) to collect, analyze, and visualize spatial data.

    o **GIS**: Combines layers of spatial data to analyze patterns and relationships.

    o **Remote Sensing**: The use of satellite or aerial imagery to monitor and analyze environmental changes.

- **Spatial Analysis**: The examination of spatial relationships and patterns, often using quantitative methods.

    o **Demographic Analysis**: Understanding population characteristics and trends.

    o **Environmental Impact Assessment**: Evaluating the potential effects of human activities on the environment.

Practical Applications

Understanding geography is essential for addressing global challenges and making informed decisions:

- **Environmental Management**: Applying geographical knowledge to conserve natural resources, manage ecosystems, and mitigate environmental issues such as climate change and deforestation.

- **Urban Planning**: Designing sustainable cities that balance growth with environmental and social considerations.

- **Disaster Management**: Using geographical tools to predict, prepare for, and respond to natural disasters like earthquakes, hurricanes, and floods.

- **Economic Development**: Analyzing spatial patterns of economic activities to promote balanced regional development and address inequalities.

Practice Problems

To reinforce your understanding of geographical concepts, solve these practice problems:

1. **Map Reading**: Interpret a topographic map to determine the elevation of a specific point.

   o Solution: Use the contour lines on the map to identify the elevation of the point, considering the contour interval provided.

2. **Climate Zones**: Describe the characteristics of the tropical rainforest biome.

   o Solution: Tropical rainforests have high temperatures, high humidity, and significant rainfall throughout the year. They are known for their dense vegetation and high biodiversity.

3. **Urbanization**: Explain the concept of urban sprawl and its potential impacts.

   o Solution: Urban sprawl refers to the uncontrolled expansion of urban areas into rural regions. It can lead to habitat loss, increased traffic congestion, and higher infrastructure costs.

4. **Population Density**: Calculate the population density of a city with a population of 1,000,000 people and an area of 500 square kilometers.

   o Solution: Population density = population/area = 1,000,000/500 = 2,000 people per square kilometer.

Civics and Government

Understanding civics and government is crucial for recognizing the structures and functions of government, as well as the rights and responsibilities of citizens. This section will cover the foundational concepts of civics and government, including the principles of democracy, the structure of the U.S. government, the functions of its branches, and the importance of civic engagement. We will also explore how these concepts apply to other governmental systems around the world.

Key Concepts in Civics and Government

Principles of Democracy

Democracy is a system of government where power is vested in the people, who exercise that power through elected representatives. Key principles of democracy include:

- **Popular Sovereignty**: The idea that the authority of the government is created and sustained by the consent of its people, through their elected representatives.

- **Rule of Law**: The principle that all members of society, including government officials, are subject to the law.

- **Individual Rights**: The protection of individual liberties and rights, such as freedom of speech, religion, and the press.

- **Majority Rule with Minority Rights**: The majority's decisions must be respected, but the rights of the minority must be protected.

Structure of the U.S. Government

The U.S. government is based on the Constitution, which outlines the structure and powers of the government. It is divided into three branches to ensure a system of checks and balances:

- **Legislative Branch**: Comprised of the Congress, which is divided into the Senate and the House of Representatives.

  - **Senate**: Each state is represented by two senators, serving six-year terms.

  - **House of Representatives**: Members are elected based on population, serving two-year terms.

  - **Functions**: The legislative branch is responsible for making laws, declaring war, regulating interstate and foreign commerce, and controlling taxing and spending policies.

- **Executive Branch**: Headed by the President, who serves a four-year term and can be re-elected for one additional term.

  - o **Vice President**: Assists the President and can become President if the current President is unable to serve.

  - o **Cabinet**: Composed of the heads of the executive departments, who advise the President.

  - o **Functions**: The executive branch enforces laws, conducts foreign policy, commands the armed forces, and oversees federal agencies.

- **Judicial Branch**: Consists of the Supreme Court and lower federal courts.

  - o **Supreme Court**: The highest court in the United States, composed of nine justices appointed for life.

  - o **Lower Courts**: Include district courts and courts of appeals.

  - o **Functions**: The judicial branch interprets laws, reviews lower court decisions, and ensures laws are consistent with the Constitution.

Functions of Government

Governments serve various functions essential for maintaining order and protecting the welfare of their citizens:

- **Maintaining Order**: Governments create and enforce laws to ensure social order and safety.

- **Providing Public Services**: Governments offer services that individuals cannot easily provide for themselves, such as education, healthcare, and infrastructure.

- **Ensuring National Security**: Governments protect the nation from external threats through military and diplomatic means.

- **Managing the Economy**: Governments regulate economic activities to promote stability and growth, including managing currency, trade, and taxation.

- **Protecting Individual Rights**: Governments safeguard the freedoms and rights of individuals, ensuring equality and justice.

Civic Engagement and Responsibilities

Citizens play a crucial role in a democracy through active participation in the political process. Key aspects of civic engagement include:

- **Voting**: One of the most fundamental rights and responsibilities of citizens. Voting allows individuals to influence government policies and leadership.

- **Participation in Civic Organizations**: Engaging in community groups, advocacy organizations, and other civic groups helps address local and national issues.

- **Public Discourse**: Staying informed about current events and engaging in discussions about public policy and societal issues.

- **Volunteering and Community Service**: Contributing time and resources to improve the community and help those in need.

- **Understanding and Respecting the Law**: Knowing the laws and the rights guaranteed by the Constitution, and adhering to them.

Comparative Government

While the U.S. government operates on democratic principles, different countries employ various forms of government. Key types include:

- **Monarchy**: A government led by a king or queen, where power may be absolute or constitutional.

  o **Absolute Monarchy**: The monarch has almost complete control, such as in Saudi Arabia.

  o **Constitutional Monarchy**: The monarch's powers are limited by a constitution, such as in the United Kingdom.

- **Authoritarian Regimes**: Governments where power is concentrated in the hands of a single leader or small group, with limited political freedoms.

  o **Examples**: North Korea, Cuba.

- **Communist States**: Governments that seek to create a classless society through state ownership of property and means of production.

  o **Examples**: China, Vietnam.

- **Republics**: Governments where the head of state is elected, and the country is considered a public matter.

  o **Examples**: United States, France.

Practical Applications

Understanding civics and government is essential for informed citizenship and effective participation in the political process. It helps individuals:

- **Make Informed Decisions**: Knowledge of government structures and functions enables citizens to make educated choices in elections and public policy debates.

- **Advocate for Change**: Understanding how government works empowers individuals to advocate for policy changes and hold elected officials accountable.

- **Protect Rights**: Awareness of individual rights and legal protections helps citizens defend their freedoms and those of others.

Practice Problems

To reinforce your understanding of civics and government concepts, solve these practice problems:

1. **Separation of Powers**: Explain how the system of checks and balances works in the U.S. government.

   o Solution: The system of checks and balances ensures that no single branch of government becomes too powerful. Each branch has specific powers that allow it to check the actions of the other branches. For example, the President can veto legislation, Congress can override a veto, and the Supreme Court can declare laws unconstitutional.

2. **Voting Rights**: Describe the significance of the 19th Amendment to the U.S. Constitution.

   o Solution: The 19th Amendment, ratified in 1920, granted women the right to vote, marking a significant expansion of voting rights and promoting gender equality in the democratic process.

3. **Functions of Government**: Identify the primary function of the legislative branch.

   o Solution: The primary function of the legislative branch is to make laws. This includes drafting, debating, and passing legislation that governs the country.

By mastering these civics and government concepts and practicing regularly, you will develop the skills needed to analyze and interpret governmental functions confidently and accurately. Next, we will explore Economics, where you will learn to understand economic principles and their applications in everyday life.

Economics

Economics is the study of how individuals, businesses, and governments allocate resources to satisfy their needs and wants. It examines the production, distribution, and consumption of goods and services, and analyzes how these activities are influenced by various factors, including market conditions, government policies, and global events. Understanding economics is crucial for making informed decisions in both personal and professional contexts. This section provides a comprehensive overview of key economic principles, systems, and policies.

Key Concepts in Economics

Basic Economic Principles

Economics is built on several foundational principles that help explain how markets function and how economic agents make decisions:

- **Scarcity**: The fundamental economic problem of having limited resources to meet unlimited wants. Scarcity forces individuals and societies to make choices about how to allocate resources efficiently.

- **Opportunity Cost**: The cost of forgoing the next best alternative when making a decision. It represents the value of the best alternative that is not chosen.

- **Supply and Demand**: The relationship between the quantity of a good or service that producers are willing to sell at various prices and the quantity that consumers are willing to buy.

  - **Law of Demand**: As the price of a good decreases, the quantity demanded increases, and vice versa.

  - **Law of Supply**: As the price of a good increases, the quantity supplied increases, and vice versa.

- **Equilibrium**: The point at which the quantity supplied equals the quantity demanded, resulting in a stable market price.

Economic Systems

Different societies use various economic systems to manage their resources and distribute goods and services:

- **Traditional Economy**: An economic system based on customs, traditions, and beliefs. Economic decisions are made according to historical patterns and cultural practices.

  - **Example**: Indigenous communities that rely on subsistence farming and bartering.

- **Command Economy**: An economic system where the government makes all economic decisions and controls the factors of production.

  o **Example**: The former Soviet Union.

- **Market Economy**: An economic system where decisions are made by individuals and businesses based on supply and demand. Prices are determined by market forces.

  o **Example**: The United States.

- **Mixed Economy**: A combination of market and command economies, where both the government and private sector play significant roles in economic decision-making.

  o **Example**: Most modern economies, including those of Canada and many European countries.

Macroeconomics vs. Microeconomics

Economics can be divided into two main branches:

- **Macroeconomics**: The study of the economy as a whole, focusing on broad issues such as national income, unemployment, inflation, and economic growth.

  o **Gross Domestic Product (GDP)**: A measure of the total value of goods and services produced within a country.

  o **Unemployment Rate**: The percentage of the labor force that is unemployed and actively seeking employment.

  o **Inflation**: The rate at which the general level of prices for goods and services rises, eroding purchasing power.

  o **Fiscal Policy**: Government actions involving taxation and spending to influence the economy.

  o **Monetary Policy**: Central bank actions to control the money supply and interest rates to stabilize the economy.

- **Microeconomics**: The study of individual economic units, such as households, businesses, and industries. It focuses on how these entities make decisions and interact in specific markets.

  o **Consumer Behavior**: How individuals make decisions about what goods and services to purchase based on their preferences and budget constraints.

  o **Production and Costs**: How businesses decide on the quantity of goods to produce and at what cost.

  o **Market Structures**: Different types of markets, including perfect competition, monopolistic competition, oligopoly, and monopoly.

International Trade

International trade involves the exchange of goods and services between countries, influenced by comparative advantage, trade policies, and global economic conditions:

- **Comparative Advantage**: The ability of a country to produce a good or service at a lower opportunity cost than another country. This principle underlies the benefits of trade.

- **Trade Policies**: Governments use tariffs, quotas, and trade agreements to regulate international trade.

  - **Tariffs**: Taxes on imported goods that make them more expensive and less competitive compared to domestic products.

  - **Quotas**: Limits on the quantity of a good that can be imported, protecting domestic industries from foreign competition.

  - **Free Trade Agreements**: Agreements between countries to reduce trade barriers and promote increased trade, such as NAFTA (North American Free Trade Agreement) and the EU (European Union) single market.

Economic Indicators

Economic indicators provide data on the health of an economy, helping policymakers, businesses, and individuals make informed decisions:

- **Gross Domestic Product (GDP)**: Measures the total value of all goods and services produced within a country over a specific period.

- **Unemployment Rate**: Indicates the percentage of the labor force that is unemployed and seeking work.

- **Inflation Rate**: Measures the rate at which the general level of prices for goods and services is rising.

- **Consumer Price Index (CPI)**: Tracks changes in the price level of a basket of consumer goods and services.

- **Interest Rates**: The cost of borrowing money, set by central banks to influence economic activity.

Practical Applications

Understanding economics is essential for making informed personal and professional decisions:

- **Personal Finance**: Knowledge of economic principles helps individuals make better decisions about saving, investing, borrowing, and budgeting.

- **Business Strategy**: Businesses use economic analysis to make decisions about production, pricing, market entry, and investment.

- **Public Policy**: Policymakers rely on economic data and theories to design effective policies that promote economic stability and growth.

- **Global Awareness**: Understanding international trade and economic indicators helps individuals and businesses navigate the global economy.

Practice Problems

To reinforce your understanding of economic concepts, solve these practice problems:

1. **Supply and Demand**: Explain how an increase in the price of a substitute good affects the demand for a product.

   o Solution: An increase in the price of a substitute good (e.g., tea) will increase the demand for the product (e.g., coffee) as consumers switch to the relatively cheaper alternative.

2. **GDP Calculation**: Calculate the GDP given the following data: consumption = $1,000 billion, investment = $500 billion, government spending = $300 billion, and net exports = -$100 billion.

   o Solution: GDP = consumption + investment + government spending + net exports = $1,000 billion + $500 billion + $300 billion - $100 billion = $1,700 billion.

3. **Comparative Advantage**: Country A can produce 10 units of product X or 20 units of product Y with the same resources. Country B can produce 15 units of product X or 15 units of product Y with the same resources. Which country has a comparative advantage in producing product Y?

   o Solution: Country A has a comparative advantage in producing product Y because it has a lower opportunity cost (1 unit of X for 2 units of Y) compared to Country B (1 unit of X for 1 unit of Y).

By mastering these economic concepts and practicing regularly, you will develop the skills needed to analyze and interpret economic data confidently and accurately. Next, we will explore Sample Questions and Answer Explanations, where you will practice applying these skills in a test-like environment and learn from detailed explanations.

Sample Questions and Answer Explanations

Practicing with sample questions and understanding their explanations is an essential part of preparing for the Social Studies section of the GED test. This approach helps you familiarize yourself with the types of questions you will encounter, improve your problem-solving skills, and build confidence. In this section, we provide a variety of sample questions from each domain covered in this chapter, followed by detailed explanations of the answers, to help you master the concepts.

Sample Question 1: U.S. History

Question: Which event marked the end of the American Civil War?

A. The Battle of Gettysburg B. The Emancipation Proclamation C. The assassination of Abraham Lincoln D. The surrender at Appomattox Court House

Answer: D. The surrender at Appomattox Court House

Explanation: The American Civil War effectively ended with the surrender of Confederate General Robert E. Lee to Union General Ulysses S. Grant at Appomattox Court House on April 9, 1865. This event marked the conclusion of major hostilities, leading to the eventual restoration of the Union.

Sample Question 2: World History

Question: Which of the following was a primary cause of World War I?

A. The rise of fascism B. The assassination of Archduke Franz Ferdinand C. The signing of the Treaty of Versailles D. The attack on Pearl Harbor

Answer: B. The assassination of Archduke Franz Ferdinand

Explanation: The assassination of Archduke Franz Ferdinand of Austria-Hungary on June 28, 1914, was the immediate catalyst for World War I. This event set off a chain reaction of alliances and conflicts, leading to the outbreak of war.

Sample Question 3: Geography

Question: Which climate zone is characterized by high temperatures and heavy rainfall throughout the year?

A. Tundra B. Desert C. Tropical rainforest D. Mediterranean

Answer: C. Tropical rainforest

Explanation: Tropical rainforest climates are characterized by consistently high temperatures and significant rainfall throughout the year. These regions are known for their dense vegetation and high biodiversity.

Sample Question 4: Civics and Government

Question: What is the primary function of the legislative branch of the U.S. government?

A. To enforce laws B. To interpret laws C. To make laws D. To conduct foreign policy

Answer: C. To make laws

Explanation: The primary function of the legislative branch, comprised of the Congress (Senate and House of Representatives), is to make laws. This includes drafting, debating, and passing legislation that governs the country.

Sample Question 5: Economics

Question: If the price of a product increases, what is likely to happen to the quantity demanded for that product, assuming all other factors remain constant?

A. The quantity demanded will increase. B. The quantity demanded will decrease. C. The quantity demanded will remain the same. D. The quantity demanded will fluctuate randomly.

Answer: B. The quantity demanded will decrease.

Explanation: According to the law of demand, there is an inverse relationship between price and quantity demanded. As the price of a product increases, the quantity demanded decreases, assuming all other factors remain constant.

Sample Question 6: Analyzing Documents and Data

Question: Given the following data table, what is the percentage increase in the population of City B from 2010 to 2020?

City	Population (2010)	Population (2020)
City A	500,000	600,000
City B	300,000	450,000
City C	400,000	500,000

A. 33% B. 50% C. 75% D. 100%

Answer: B. 50%

Explanation: The percentage increase in population is calculated as follows: Percentage Increase = [(Population in 2020 - Population in 2010)/Population in 2010] * 100 For City B: [(450,000 - 300,000)/300,000] * 100 = 50%

Sample Question 7: Interpreting Graphs and Tables

Question: Refer to the following bar graph showing the annual sales of four products (A, B, C, D) in a store. Which product had the highest sales?

- **Title**: Annual Sales of Products
- **X-Axis**: Products (A, B, C, D)
- **Y-Axis**: Sales (units)

A. Product A B. Product B C. Product C D. Product D

Answer: B. Product B

Explanation: By examining the bar graph, it is clear that Product B has the tallest bar, indicating it had the highest sales among the four products.

Sample Question 8: Comparative Government

Question: Which of the following countries operates as a constitutional monarchy?

A. Saudi Arabia B. North Korea C. United Kingdom D. China

Answer: C. United Kingdom

Explanation: The United Kingdom operates as a constitutional monarchy, where the monarch's powers are limited by a constitution and elected parliamentary bodies govern the country.

Sample Question 9: Macroeconomics

Question: What is the primary goal of monetary policy?

A. To control inflation and stabilize the currency B. To increase government spending C. To reduce taxation D. To regulate international trade

Answer: A. To control inflation and stabilize the currency

Explanation: The primary goal of monetary policy, conducted by a country's central bank, is to control inflation and stabilize the currency. This is achieved by managing interest rates and regulating the money supply.

Sample Question 10: Microeconomics

Question: If a firm faces decreasing marginal costs of production, what will happen to the cost of producing additional units of output?

A. The cost will increase. B. The cost will decrease. C. The cost will remain constant. D. The cost will fluctuate unpredictably.

Answer: B. The cost will decrease.

Explanation: Decreasing marginal costs of production mean that as the firm produces more units, the cost of producing each additional unit decreases. This often occurs due to economies of scale and increased efficiency.

By practicing these sample questions and thoroughly understanding the explanations, you will strengthen your ability to apply social studies concepts and interpret data effectively. Regular practice with a variety of problems helps solidify your understanding and improves your ability to analyze and answer questions accurately. Next, we will explore Analyzing Documents and Data, where you will learn to critically evaluate various types of information sources and draw meaningful conclusions.

CHAPTER 7
FULL LENGTH PRACTICE TESTS

| Practice Test | Online Test Simulation

To provide a superior exam simulation experience, all ten full-length practice exams are available exclusively on our online platform. This immersive approach offers you the chance to practice in an environment closely mirroring the actual GED exam.

Benefits of Using Our Online Test Simulation Platform:

1. **Realistic Exam Experience:** Our platform mimics the actual GED exam format, helping you get accustomed to the test structure and timing, ensuring you are well-prepared for exam day.

2. **Instant Feedback:** Receive immediate explanations for incorrect answers, helping you understand the correct responses and learn from your mistakes instantly.

3. **Comprehensive Practice:** With eight additional practice exams, you can significantly expand your test-taking practice, covering all key topics and question types on the GED exam.

4. **Progress Tracking:** Track your progress over time, review scores, identify areas for improvement, and adjust your study plan accordingly. This personalized approach enhances your overall performance.

5. **Flexible Learning:** Take online exams at your convenience, fitting practice sessions into your schedule without constraints, allowing you to study and practice at your own pace.

6. **Enhanced Learning Experience:** Benefit from instant feedback, detailed explanations, and the ability to review answers, enhancing your understanding of difficult questions and complex concepts.

▍Accessing the Online Exam Simulator

1. **Scan the QR Code**:

2. **Access the Platform**:
   - The link will direct you to our online exam simulator platform.

3. **Taking the Exam:** Each practice exam is timed and designed to simulate the real GED exam environment. Answer questions to the best of your ability and receive instant explanations for incorrect answers.

4. **Review and Track Your Progress:** After completing each exam, review your answers and see detailed explanations for all questions. Use the progress tracking feature to monitor your improvement over time and identify areas needing further practice.

By integrating these online resources into your study plan, you can maximize your preparation and boost your confidence for the GED exam. Our goal is to provide you with the tools and support needed to achieve success for your GED exam. Embark on your journey to GED success with our comprehensive online test simulation platform. Together, we'll ensure that you are fully equipped to conquer the GED exam and advance your education and career.

CHAPTER 8
HOW TO OVERCOME TEST ANXIETY

Test anxiety is a common challenge that many students face, often hindering their performance despite adequate preparation. This chapter is dedicated to understanding the nature of test anxiety and providing practical strategies to manage and overcome it. By addressing both short-term techniques for staying calm during the exam and long-term strategies for managing anxiety, this chapter aims to equip you with the tools needed to perform your best on test day.

Test anxiety manifests in various ways, including physical symptoms like sweating and increased heart rate, cognitive issues such as negative thoughts and difficulty concentrating, and emotional reactions like fear and helplessness. Understanding these symptoms is the first step in managing anxiety effectively.

In this section, we will explore tips for staying calm during the exam, such as breathing exercises, positive visualization, and effective time management. These techniques can help you maintain focus and reduce stress in the moment. Following this, we will delve into long-term anxiety management strategies, including developing a consistent study routine, practicing mindfulness, and seeking professional help if needed. These strategies aim to build resilience and reduce overall anxiety levels over time.

By implementing the techniques outlined in this chapter, you can transform your test-taking experience from one of dread to one of confidence and control. Let's begin by examining the immediate steps you can take to stay calm during the exam.

Tips for Staying Calm During the Exam

Feeling anxious during an exam is normal, but it's crucial to manage this anxiety to ensure it doesn't negatively impact your performance. Here are several effective strategies to help you stay calm during the exam:

1. **Deep Breathing Exercises:** Deep breathing is a simple yet powerful technique to reduce anxiety. When you feel anxious, your breathing becomes shallow and rapid. To counter this, take a few moments to breathe deeply. Inhale slowly through your nose, hold your breath for a few seconds, and then exhale slowly through your mouth. Repeat this process several times to help calm your mind and body.

2. **Positive Visualization:** Visualization involves picturing a positive outcome in your mind. Before and during the exam, take a moment to close your eyes and visualize yourself successfully completing the test. Imagine feeling confident and relaxed as you answer each question. This positive imagery can boost your confidence and reduce anxiety.

3. **Effective Time Management:** Managing your time effectively during the exam can prevent panic and ensure you have enough time to answer all questions. Start by quickly scanning the entire test to get an idea of the types and number of questions. Allocate time based on the marks assigned to each section, and keep an eye on the clock. If you encounter a difficult question, move on and return to it later if time permits.

4. **Stay Focused on the Present:** Avoid thinking about the outcome of the test or comparing yourself to other test-takers. Concentrate on one question at a time and stay in the present moment. If your mind starts to wander, gently bring your focus back to the task at hand.

5. **Physical Relaxation Techniques:** Simple physical exercises can also help reduce anxiety. Try gently tensing and then relaxing different muscle groups in your body, starting from your toes and working your way up to your head. This can help release physical tension and promote a sense of calm.

6. **Positive Self-Talk:** Replace negative thoughts with positive affirmations. Instead of thinking, "I can't do this," tell yourself, "I am well-prepared and capable." Remind yourself of your strengths and past successes.

By incorporating these techniques, you can create a calm and focused mindset during the exam, allowing you to perform to the best of your abilities.

Long-Term Anxiety Management Strategies

Managing test anxiety effectively requires not only short-term techniques for staying calm during the exam but also long-term strategies to build resilience and reduce overall anxiety levels. By incorporating these strategies into your daily routine, you can develop a stronger, more confident mindset that will benefit you not only in test situations but in all areas of life.

1. Develop a Consistent Study Routine

A well-structured study routine can significantly reduce anxiety by ensuring you are well-prepared for the test. Set aside dedicated study time each day and stick to it. Break your study sessions into manageable chunks with regular breaks to avoid burnout. Use tools like planners or apps to organize your study schedule and keep track of your progress. A consistent routine helps you build familiarity with the material, making you feel more confident and less anxious as the test day approaches.

2. Practice Mindfulness and Relaxation Techniques

Mindfulness involves being present in the moment and fully engaging with your current activity without judgment. Incorporating mindfulness practices, such as meditation, yoga, or deep breathing exercises, into your daily routine can help reduce anxiety over time. Regular practice of these techniques helps train your mind to stay calm and focused, even in stressful situations. Apps like Headspace or Calm offer guided meditations that can help you get started with mindfulness practice.

3. Maintain a Healthy Lifestyle

Your physical health significantly impacts your mental well-being. Ensure you get enough sleep, eat a balanced diet, and engage in regular physical activity. Exercise, in particular, is known to reduce anxiety and improve mood by releasing endorphins. Aim for at least 30 minutes of moderate exercise most days of the week. Staying hydrated and avoiding excessive caffeine and sugar can also help keep anxiety levels in check.

4. Positive Self-Talk and Visualization

Cultivating a positive mindset can help reduce long-term anxiety. Practice positive self-talk by replacing negative thoughts with encouraging ones. Instead of focusing on potential failures, remind yourself of your strengths and past successes. Visualization is another powerful tool. Regularly visualize yourself succeeding in the test, feeling calm and confident. This mental rehearsal can help create a positive expectation and reduce anxiety.

5. Build a Support System

Having a strong support system can make a significant difference in managing anxiety. Surround yourself with supportive friends, family, or peers who understand your goals and can offer encouragement. Discussing your anxieties with someone you trust can provide relief and help you gain perspective. Consider joining a study group where you can share resources, discuss difficult topics, and motivate each other.

6. Seek Professional Help if Needed

If anxiety becomes overwhelming and interferes with your daily life, consider seeking help from a mental health professional. Therapists can provide you with additional strategies and coping mechanisms tailored to your specific needs. Cognitive-behavioral therapy (CBT) is particularly effective for managing anxiety, as it helps you identify and change negative thought patterns and behaviors.

7. Gradual Exposure to Test Conditions

Gradual exposure to test conditions can help desensitize you to the anxiety associated with exams. Take practice tests under timed conditions similar to the actual exam. Familiarize yourself with the test format, question types, and time constraints. The more you practice in a simulated test environment, the more comfortable and confident you will become.

8. Establish a Pre-Test Routine

Developing a pre-test routine can help reduce anxiety on the day of the exam. Create a checklist of activities that help you feel prepared and relaxed, such as reviewing key notes, engaging in light exercise, or practicing deep breathing. Stick to this routine to create a sense of control and familiarity, which can help calm your nerves.

By integrating these long-term strategies into your daily life, you can build a solid foundation for managing anxiety. These practices not only help reduce test anxiety but also promote overall mental and physical well-being. Consistency is key—over time, these strategies will help you develop resilience and confidence, enabling you to approach tests and other challenges with a calm and focused mindset.

CHAPTER 9
APPENDIX

Glossary of Terms

This glossary is designed to provide clear and concise definitions of key terms and concepts that appear throughout this book. Understanding these terms will help you navigate the material more effectively and enhance your overall comprehension. Each term is defined in the context of its relevance to the GED test and the subjects it covers.

A

- **Absolute Value**: The distance of a number from zero on the number line, regardless of direction. For example, the absolute value of -5 is 5.

- **Algebra**: A branch of mathematics that uses symbols and letters to represent numbers and quantities in formulas and equations.

B

- **Bias**: A tendency to lean in a certain direction, often to the detriment of an objective viewpoint. Bias can affect the fairness and accuracy of information.

- **Biome**: A large naturally occurring community of flora and fauna occupying a major habitat, e.g., forest or tundra.

C

- **Circumference**: The distance around the edge of a circle. It can be calculated using the formula $C = 2\pi r$, where r is the radius of the circle.

- **Civic Duty**: Responsibilities of a citizen, including voting, obeying laws, and serving on juries.

D

- **Data**: Facts and statistics collected for reference or analysis. In the context of the GED, data is often presented in graphs, tables, or charts.

- **Democracy**: A system of government where the citizens exercise power by voting. It is characterized by fair and free elections, the rule of law, and protection of human rights.

E

- **Ecosystem**: A biological community of interacting organisms and their physical environment. It includes both biotic (living) and abiotic (non-living) components.

- **Equation**: A mathematical statement that asserts the equality of two expressions, typically written in the form of 'A = B'.

F

- **Fraction**: A numerical quantity that is not a whole number, representing a part of a whole. It is written in the form a/b, where a is the numerator and b is the denominator.

- **Function**: A relationship or expression involving one or more variables. In mathematics, a function defines a particular output for each input.

G

- **Genotype**: The genetic constitution of an individual organism. It is the set of genes in our DNA responsible for a particular trait.

- **Graph**: A diagram representing a system of connections or interrelations among two or more things by a number of distinctive dots, lines, bars, etc.

H

- **Hypothesis**: A proposed explanation for a phenomenon, used as a starting point for further investigation. It must be testable and falsifiable.

- **Human Rights**: Fundamental rights and freedoms to which all humans are entitled, such as freedom of speech and religion.

I

- **Inequality**: A mathematical statement that indicates one quantity is larger or smaller than another, expressed with symbols such as $>$, $<$, $\geq$, or $\leq$.

- **Inference**: A conclusion reached based on evidence and reasoning. In reading comprehension, it involves deriving logical conclusions from the text.

J

- **Judicial Branch**: The part of the government responsible for interpreting laws and administering justice. In the U.S., this includes the Supreme Court and other federal courts.

K

- **Kinetic Energy**: The energy possessed by an object due to its motion. It is calculated as $KE = 1/2 mv^2$, where m is mass and v is velocity.

L

- **Latitude**: The angular distance of a place north or south of the earth's equator, typically measured in degrees.

- **Legislature**: A governmental body with the power to make, amend, and repeal laws.

M

- **Median**: The middle value in a list of numbers. If the list has an even number of entries, the median is the average of the two middle numbers.

- **Molecule**: The smallest unit of a chemical compound that can exist; composed of two or more atoms held together by chemical bonds.

N

- **Narrative**: A spoken or written account of connected events; a story. In literature, it refers to the structured sequence of events in a text.

- **Neuron**: A specialized cell transmitting nerve impulses; a nerve cell.

O

- **Osmosis**: The process by which molecules of a solvent pass through a semipermeable membrane from a less concentrated solution into a more concentrated one, equalizing the concentrations on both sides.

- **Oxidation**: A chemical reaction in which a substance loses electrons, often associated with gaining oxygen or losing hydrogen.

P

- **Parliament**: The highest legislative authority in a country. In some countries, it is the equivalent of Congress.

- **Photosynthesis**: The process by which green plants and some other organisms use sunlight to synthesize foods from carbon dioxide and water.

Q

- **Quadratic Equation**: A second-order polynomial equation in a single variable, typically written as $ax^2 + bx + c = 0$.

- **Qualitative Data**: Information that describes qualities or characteristics, often collected through observations.

R

- **Radius**: A straight line from the center to the circumference of a circle or sphere.

CHAPTER 9
APPENDIX

- **Revolution**: A forcible overthrow of a government or social order in favor of a new system. Also, the movement of an object in a circular or elliptical course around another or about an axis or center.

S

- **Synthesis**: The combination of components or elements to form a connected whole, particularly in chemistry where simpler substances combine to form more complex ones.
- **Symbiosis**: Interaction between two different organisms living in close physical association, typically to the advantage of both.

T

- **Theorem**: A general proposition not self-evident but proved by a chain of reasoning; a truth established by means of accepted truths.
- **Tropism**: The orientation of an organism to an external stimulus, such as light or gravity.

U

- **Universe**: All existing matter and space considered as a whole; the cosmos.
- **Urbanization**: The process of making an area more urban, typically involving an increase in population and infrastructure.

V

- **Variable**: An element, feature, or factor that is liable to vary or change. In mathematics, a symbol used to represent a number in expressions or equations.
- **Velocity**: The speed of something in a given direction.

W

- **Wavelength**: The distance between successive crests of a wave, especially points in a sound wave or electromagnetic wave.
- **Water Cycle**: The cycle of processes by which water circulates between the earth's oceans, atmosphere, and land, involving precipitation, drainage, and return to the atmosphere by evaporation and transpiration.

X

- **X-axis**: The horizontal axis in a coordinate plane.

Y

- **Y-axis**: The vertical axis in a coordinate plane.

Z

- **Zygote**: A eukaryotic cell formed by a fertilization event between two gametes.

Study Plan Templates

Creating an effective study plan is crucial for organizing your time, covering all necessary material, and ensuring you are well-prepared for the GED test. In this section, we provide templates to help you structure your study sessions. These templates are designed to be flexible and adaptable to your personal schedule and study preferences.

4-Week Study Plan Template

This 4-week study plan is designed to help you systematically cover all the subjects tested on the GED. Each week focuses on specific subjects and includes time for review and practice tests.

Week 1: Reasoning Through Language Arts (RLA)

- **Day 1:**
    - Read and annotate two reading passages.
    - Practice identifying main ideas and supporting details.
    - Review grammar rules and complete practice exercises.

- **Day 2:**
    - Write a short essay response to a given prompt.
    - Practice sentence structure and paragraph organization.
    - Review vocabulary and word usage.

- **Day 3:**
    - Read two more passages and answer comprehension questions.
    - Focus on writing mechanics: punctuation, capitalization, and spelling.
    - Review previous day's work and make corrections.

- **Day 4:**
    - Take a practice RLA test.
    - Review incorrect answers and understand the rationale behind the correct answers.

- **Day 5:**
    - Review essay writing techniques.
    - Write another essay response.
    - Practice time management skills by timing yourself on practice questions.

- **Day 6:**
    - ○ Engage in extended reading: read a longer article or a book chapter.
    - ○ Summarize the content and discuss its main themes and ideas.
- **Day 7:**
    - ○ Rest day or light review: go over flashcards or review notes.

Week 2: Mathematical Reasoning

- **Day 1:**
    - ○ Review basic arithmetic: addition, subtraction, multiplication, division.
    - ○ Practice problems involving fractions and decimals.
- **Day 2:**
    - ○ Study algebra: solving equations and inequalities.
    - ○ Practice with algebraic expressions and word problems.
- **Day 3:**
    - ○ Focus on geometry: properties of shapes, area, perimeter, volume.
    - ○ Solve geometry problems and review formulas.
- **Day 4:**
    - ○ Practice data analysis: interpreting graphs, tables, and charts.
    - ○ Work on probability and statistics problems.
- **Day 5:**
    - ○ Take a practice math test.
    - ○ Review incorrect answers and understand the rationale behind the correct answers.
- **Day 6:**
    - ○ Study advanced topics: functions, quadratic equations, and polynomials.
    - ○ Practice solving higher-level math problems.
- **Day 7:**
    - ○ Rest day or light review: go over flashcards or review notes.

Week 3: Science

- **Day 1:**
    - ○ Review basic concepts in life science: cell structure, genetics, evolution.
    - ○ Practice interpreting scientific texts and diagrams.

- **Day 2:**
  - o Study physical science: laws of motion, energy, waves.
  - o Solve problems related to physical science concepts.

- **Day 3:**
  - o Focus on earth and space science: geology, meteorology, astronomy.
  - o Practice with earth and space science questions.

- **Day 4:**
  - o Review scientific methods and practices: experiments, data analysis.
  - o Practice interpreting experimental results and scientific data.

- **Day 5:**
  - o Take a practice science test.
  - o Review incorrect answers and understand the rationale behind the correct answers.

- **Day 6:**
  - o Engage in hands-on science activities or experiments.
  - o Reflect on the scientific concepts involved in the activities.

- **Day 7:**
  - o Rest day or light review: go over flashcards or review notes.

Week 4: Social Studies

- **Day 1:**
  - o Review U.S. history: major events, important figures, and historical documents.
  - o Practice interpreting historical texts and primary sources.

- **Day 2:**
  - o Study world history: significant events and civilizations.
  - o Work on timeline exercises and map-based questions.

- **Day 3:**
  - o Focus on civics and government: structure of government, constitutional principles, and citizen responsibilities.
  - o Practice with civics-related questions and scenarios.

- **Day 4:**

- o Review economics: basic economic principles, market structures, and financial literacy.

- o Solve problems related to economic concepts.

- **Day 5:**

  - o Take a practice social studies test.

  - o Review incorrect answers and understand the rationale behind the correct answers.

- **Day 6:**

  - o Engage in current events analysis: read articles or watch news segments and discuss their social studies implications.

- **Day 7:**

  - o Rest day or light review: go over flashcards or review notes.

Daily Study Plan Template

For more flexible daily study sessions, use this template to plan your activities:

- **Morning Session:**

  - o Review notes from the previous day.

  - o Study new material for one subject (e.g., RLA, Math, Science, Social Studies).

- **Afternoon Session:**

  - o Take practice quizzes or solve problems related to the morning's study material.

  - o Engage in interactive activities, such as group study or educational games.

- **Evening Session:**

  - o Review the day's work and summarize key points.

  - o Read a related article or watch a video to reinforce learning.

Weekly Review Plan

At the end of each week, review the material covered:

- **Saturday:**

  - o Review all notes and summaries from the week.

  - o Identify areas of strength and weakness.

  - o Plan next week's focus based on this review.

- **Sunday:**
  - Rest and recharge, or engage in light review activities.

Using these templates, you can create a personalized study plan that fits your schedule and learning style. Consistency and regular review are key to retaining information and building confidence for the GED test. Good luck with your studies!

Made in the USA
Monee, IL
17 June 2025